Dear Dissertation Writer: STORIES, STRATEGIES, & SELF-CARE TIPS TO GET DONE

By Susan D. Corbin, Ph.D.

Cover design by Karie Williams
Interior design by Roberta Morris, Leave It to 'Berta
Illustrations by Janine Dworin

Chapter 2 was in ABD Survival Guide May, 2004 in a different form

Chapter 3 was in ABD Survival Guide September, 2003 in a different form

Chapter 14 was published by Story Circle Network in December, 2019 in a different form

Dear Dissertation Writer: Stories, Strategies & Self-Care Tips to Get Done
© 2021, Susan D. Corbin, Ph.D.

ISBN: 978-1-7373325-0-3

CONTENTS

Preface 5

Section 1: First, Get Over Yourself 9
    Chapter 1: PhD Stands for 10
    Chapter 2: How to Sabotage Your Dissertation 17
    Chapter 3: Think of It This Way: It's No Big Deal! It's Lots of Small Deals!. 29
    Chapter 4: Brave Saves the Day 34
    Chapter 5: How to Lose Control 41

Section 2: Topics, Proposals, Committees, … Oh My! 49
    Chapter 6: Topic? Schmopic? Decide Already! 50
    Chapter 7: Yep, Your Fate is in Their Hands 60
    Chapter 8: Who's on First? Or What to Do First? 66
    Chapter 9: What's It Supposed to Look Like? 72

Section 3: When the Writing Muse Flips You Off 85
    Chapter 10: Shhh… Butt in Chair Time is Sacred 86
    Chapter 11: You Have to Write to Write 96
    Chapter 12: Oh, Yeah? Prove It 107

Section 4: Showtime 115
    Chapter 13: The Anxiety is Almost Over 116
    Chapter 14: My Tale of Two Committees 124
    Chapter 15: You Deserve to Celebrate! 128
    Acknowledgments 133
    About the Author 135

PREFACE

Dear Dissertation Writer,

Welcome to the book that will make writing your dissertation a breeze.

Oh, wait. If only that were true.

However, now that I have your attention, this book will be of immense help to you because it is different from other "How to Write Your Dissertation" books. The difference? I address key emotional issues first; then, address logistical issues. This book is for dissertation writers regardless of where they find themselves on the emotional continuum from feeling a bit of trepidation about starting the project to being in a total freak-out mode about writing it; whether you are just starting or halfway done. The book includes stories of composite graduate students having the problems I observed real students struggling with. What you'll find here are strategies – both emotional and logistical – to help get you out of stuck places and get to the goal line of "Done."

There are four sections in this book:

1. "First, Get Over Yourself"
2. "Topics, Proposals, Committees... Oh, My!"
3. "When the Muse Flips You Off"
4. "Show Time"

"First, Get Over Yourself" means let go of your preconceived notions of how writing a dissertation is supposed to go. Don't expect to be perfect. Faculty members don't expect it. The students I've seen who expected perfection of themselves were the ones who faltered and some failed. The stories in this book based on composite graduate students will help you understand what "getting over" yourself means and provide strategies to help you do it.

Another question "First, Get Over Yourself" addresses is, "Where do I start in this bewildering process of writing a dissertation?" Students set themselves up for failure by thinking they have to know exactly what they

are doing and not be vulnerable about their fears in starting the research or the writing. The chapters in Section 1 address these concerns by:
- ✓ Showing that fear is often present and it is okay
- ✓ Breaking the dissertation into smaller parts
- ✓ Dealing with vulnerability in presenting new ideas
- ✓ Demonstrating that there are controllable events and uncontrollable happenings

Section 2, "Topics, Proposals, Committees… Oh, My!" focuses on academic details requiring consideration. These details are issues a faculty advisor might not think to mention, such as, how to decide on a research topic; how to choose dissertation committee members; and a suggested order to writing a dissertation that may not be intuitive.

A chapter in section 3, "When the Muse Flips You Off" is a description of strategies for getting writing done and how writing improves the more it's revised. Another chapter answers a question students often don't think to ask: "Why write a dissertation in the first place?" Faculty members may not think to bring it up either. Students' thinking about writing a dissertation usually devolves into "It's the last of the hurdles to getting a doctorate." However, there is a valid and important reason, which you'll find explained there.

In Section 4, "Show Time," the chapters have discussions about the dissertation defense in general; the author's dissertation defense specifically; and, finally, why go to the university's graduation ceremony. Who would have thought that last statement was even a question, but it is. Read the chapter and come to your conclusion.

Why did I write this book? Why should I be the person to write about these things? I've written a dissertation and defended it, as discussed in Chapter 14. I know the hurdles of writing. Also since 2004, I have worked with and coached hundreds of graduate students through writing their dissertations. Coaching is a process in which the coach listens to the problems a student is having and then helps the student figure out the best way to work through the problem. When a coach offers suggestions, it's always with this understanding: the student/client can accept a coach's suggestion, reject it, or modify it with no harm done to the relationship. Often a student's relationship with a faculty member is different. When

PREFACE

a faculty advisor suggests something be done to a dissertation, it is with the understanding the student is obligated to do it.

A faculty advisor, a role I've never played, is the person to approve the literature on which students are basing their research, as well as approving their methods. Further, faculty advisors determine if the data has been mined accurately with clear conclusions presented. This is a different process than coaching students. Occasionally, faculty members coach as well as advise. If you have a coaching faculty advisor, consider yourself lucky.

Most faculty advisors are interested in seeing progress month-by-month in a student's research. As a dissertation coach, I am interested in offering you emotional support through the dissertation process. My job is to help clients and readers of this book clarify the problems they are having with their writing, which may in fact be emotionally related, such as perfectionism or concerns about what others will think. Another issue may be that your progress has slowed due to a need to discuss your argument with a knowledgeable person.

Over my years of coaching graduate students, I realized some issues might look simple to the outsider or the experienced faculty member, but are absolutely foreign and very scary to a first-time dissertator. For example, students can falsely assume that everyone in their cohort knows what they are doing. Students often wonder but are afraid to ask, "Who should be on my dissertation committee?"

Given what I know, I hated the thought I'd retire and the valuable observations I've had about writing a dissertation would disappear. I wanted to share my thoughts with more than the students with whom I would come in contact. I won't be able to personally coach every student looking for help, so I wrote this book. I hope it is of use to you.

Warmly,

Susan D. Corbin, Ph.D.
AKA Dear Dissertation Coach
@diss_coach on Twitter
September 2021

Section 1:
FIRST, GET OVER YOURSELF

Chapter 1:
PHD STANDS FOR . . .

...the only element I find common to all successful writers is persistence — and overwhelming determination to succeed.

~ **Sophy Burnham**

I was in the departmental break room when graduate student Amy Get-It-Right came in with a long face. "What's wrong?" I asked her.

"I've been working on my dissertation for months and my hypotheses seem to need more and more shoring up," she said.

"Yeah, I know," I said. "Piled higher and deeper, right?"

She smiled, straightened her shoulders, poured herself a cup of coffee, and said, "I guess I'll get back to it."

I don't know when I first heard PhD stands for Piled higher and Deeper, but I assume it has been around for a long time. There is even a comic strip by that name. More benignly, I've heard students say the three letters stand for **P**atiently **h**oping for a **D**egree.

In this chapter, I'm going to suggest some qualities for the letters P, h, and D I hope will be helpful as you work toward getting your dissertation done.

 **What do the letters PhD stand for in your life? Think of something funny.**

PHD STANDS FOR . . .

"P" stands for persistence. While writing my dissertation, I had to continually tell myself: *"The P in PhD stands for persistence."* I tell the graduate students I coach the same thing: *"Persistence is what you need to write a dissertation."* You also need three other qualities, which you already have: intelligence, knowledge, and writing skills. How do you know you have these qualities? Passing course work indicated intelligence; qualifying exams required knowledge; and course papers exemplified writing skills. The only requirement left after course work and qualifying exams is writing the dissertation, which takes, more than anything else, persistence.

Writing a dissertation is different from taking classes, exams, and research papers. In those endeavors, professors or instructors tell students what needs to be done for the paper or course. A syllabus with instructions for the assigned research includes detailed instructions. For a dissertation, you are responsible for making the major decisions. If luck prevails, your faculty advisor provides helpful support. Even with support, embarking on a dissertation project can feel like setting off into a vast landscape of unknowns with few people to tell you how to navigate it.

In the absence of a helpful and positive ranger to guide one through this landscape, many end up succumbing to a team of inner critics. I call them the "Committee in Your Head," also known in this book as CYH (looks like "sigh," doesn't it?). We all have a CYH and some are louder than others. A CYH might be so loud it drowns out rational thoughts. For others, the CYH is a niggling doubt permanently residing on the edge of their brains. The CYH becomes particularly noisy when there is uncertainty or change in life—writing a dissertation qualifies on both of those points.

The CYH will sabotage you perhaps unintentionally but absolutely. Understand the CYH's main priority is safety and protection from failure. Venturing outside your comfort zone is not safe. For example, to write a dissertation one of the first questions asked is, "What should I research?" The CYH will say, "You're out of luck. There are no new topics in the world, so it will be impossible to research an original finding." When you hear this bogus thought, recall the word persistence.

Personal questions may come up, too, such as, "Will my research be good enough?" Again, the CYH may say, "You are not smart enough. You will fail." A knowing dissertation writer upon hearing this message returns the reply—Persist.

How do you *do* persistence? Step by step. Sit down at your computer to write as often as possible, collect or enter data, find another reference, and get your faculty advisor's responses to what you have written. Keep it up and one day your dissertation will be finished.

 **In what other endeavors in your life have you shown persistence?**

"h" stands for humbling. I found writing a dissertation to be the most humbling experience of my life. There is a tremendous amount of knowledge in the world and I aimed to contribute to it, which appeared loaded with hubris to me. Who was I to contribute to scientific knowledge?

Maybe the CYH says, "Everyone else in the cohort knows what they are doing." Your faculty advisor acts as if everything is fine. Your classmates are breezing through their dissertation writing. Yet, the CYH says you have no idea how to do any dissertation activity. Stop comparing your insides to everyone else's outsides. Your faculty advisor acts as if everything is fine. Has he said that? Have you asked for feedback? Classmates appear to be doing well. Is that true? Get verifiable evidence to refute the CYH.

Reach out to others. Get help. Talk to someone who has recently finished a dissertation and they will tell you how difficult it was. Hire a coach to help break the dissertation into manageable pieces. Humbling it may be, but harken back to the "P" and remember that persistence gets it done.

DEAR DISSERTATION WRITER

"h" also stands for hard work. Even though the "h" is a lowercase letter, I'm going to ask it to do double duty. These are the five hardest things I found about writing a dissertation:

1. Dealing with the CYH fears at this level of academia.
2. Coming up with an original research topic worthy of researching and doing the research solo.
3. Building an argument or rationale.
4. Finding the right theory and previous research to support my argument.
5. Getting my butt in the chair to write.

What made graduate school hard for Amy Get-It-Right was her desire to do everything perfectly. She did not want to look bad in front of her professors, whom she thought were the best in their profession. She wanted to shine for them. When it came time for her to write a dissertation, dealing with her self-doubts was difficult.

The hardest part of writing a dissertation for Steve Social-Star, a doctoral student in Interpersonal Communication, was writing on a regular schedule. He considered "fun and exciting" to be the best parts of life. Often sitting down and writing did not fit into the category of fun and exciting. He had to create strategies for writing.

 **What will be hard and humbling tasks in writing a dissertation for you? How will you handle those tasks?**

PHD STANDS FOR . . .

"D" stands for determination. I made the humble little "h" do double duty, so I'm going to do the same for the capital "D." First, the "D" in PhD stands for determination. At the end of the book, I will share what else it means, but let's not jump ahead.

How is determination different from persistence? Determination is within you, a characteristic of your mindset. Persistence is what a person does and determination is a frame of mind. With determination, you will be persistent.

"Yeah, but where does one get determination?" asked Steve Social-Star. Sometimes it takes envisioning a future to pull you through to your goal, such as getting a job as a researcher at a first-class university in your hometown or helping first-generation students excel in a community college. Other times determination comes from your desire to accomplish the doctoral goal, that is, realizing that you want a doctorate for whatever reason – perhaps to prove to yourself you can accomplish it. There are many reasons students have for getting a doctoral degree.

 **What is your reason for getting a doctoral degree?**

Finally, the reason may be, "I've spent this long working on this degree and, by golly, and I'm going to finish it." That's determination.

 **How have you demonstrated determination in the past?**

Yes, I know I said I was going to make the "D" stand for two things. What could it be? Hold on. The big reveal will be in the last chapter.

Dear Dissertation Writer,

Please read on and discover what it will take to finish your dissertation. Your PhD will mean more than Piled higher and Deeper, I promise.

Remember:

- ❏ "P" stands for persistence.
- ❏ "h" stands for humbling and hard.
- ❏ "D" stands for determination and ?

Chapter 2:
HOW TO SABOTAGE YOUR DISSERTATION

Feel the fear and do it anyway.

~ Susan Jeffers, PhD

Ursula Uncertain and I met for our weekly coaching session.

"I feel sick to my stomach when I think of writing, so I find other things to do," she said.

"Sounds like fear might be a problem here. What do you think?" I said.

"Possibly. I am afraid of what my advisor will say if I give him something."

"Ursula, remember, fear is not a bad thing. It's a very human reaction to a challenge and writing a dissertation is a huge challenge. Having fear is an expected reaction. The question is what do you do with the fear you might be feeling."

In the above story, a graduate student discussed a symptom of fear. Here's a list of other symptoms:

❏ I find things to do other than writing.

❏ I don't remember where my dissertation computer files are.

❏ I stare at the blank page on my computer screen during writing time.

❏ The CYH (Committee in Your Head) paralyzes me with "You can't do this."

❏ I delete everything I write.

DEAR DISSERTATION WRITER

Do any of these statements ring true for you? Then fear of writing may be the reason you are not starting or finishing your dissertation.

Recognize fear or anxiety. First, as with most problems, you have to recognize you have one. The knot in your stomach when you try to write the perfect sentence is fear. It resembles the feelings you got in grade school when the bully down the street forced you to give up your lunch money instead of getting a knuckle sandwich (or maybe that was just in the Andy Griffith Show). The butterflies in your stomach when you have to do a presentation in front of an audience? Yeah, fear, again. Other parts of your body besides your stomach indicate fear or anxiety. If I'm under pressure for too long, my sternum hurts. When I catch myself rubbing my breastbone with my knuckles, I realize I'm anxious and didn't recognize it.

 **Where do you feel stress/anxiety/fear in your body?**

HOW TO SABOTAGE YOUR DISSERTATION

Even Curt Competent let anxiety stall his dissertation writing. He came to a coaching session with me laughing at himself. He said to me with a chuckle "I didn't start writing the conclusion to my dissertation until I realized I was anxious about the claims I planned to make in the chapter. Luckily, I noticed and recognized my feelings as anxiety."

"What actions did you take once you noticed that it was anxiety stalling the process?" I asked.

"I took a couple of deep breaths and went for a walk in the park. When I got back to the writing, I felt better able to handle it." Good for Curt!

Anxiety is no small experience for some people. It eats their lives and leaves no space for minor activities like dissertation writing. If anxiety is a monster in your life, I'm sorry to say this small book may not help you. I can't do the topic justice here, but there are many books out there that I hope will help you. Please see a counselor. Check to see if your university provides free counseling for students.

Are you procrastinating? You've not worked on your project in a while. Why not? It may be there are more important things going on in your life that preclude working on it. Life, death, and family issues are more important than your writing project, but cleaning your house and bathing the dog are not. Procrastinator Steve Social-Star's home had to be immaculate before he could sit down and write on his dissertation. We talked about it and he worked out a plan—if he straightened his desk, he could work without vacuuming the entire apartment first.

Fay Focused-and-Quiet did fine in her course work, but when it came to writing her dissertation, she couldn't make herself sit down. She had done a lot of research and knew what her argument was going to be. She'd think about writing and put it on her calendar. She'd sit down at her computer and get antsy like she should be doing something ... anything else.

After our discussion, Fay realized every time she sat down to write, her fear was of her master's degree advisor, who had been a very harsh critic. This fear wasn't explicit and it took her time to figure it out. Fay's dissertation advisor was supportive of reading rough drafts and offering comments to make Fay's writing better. She needed to unearth why she was still hesitant to write. Realizing that the fear of her master's advisor's critical comments was stopping her relieved the CYH's anxiety and Fay could sit down and write.

Pay attention to how your body feels when you sit down to write and the times when you can't. Do you experience the same sensations when you think about writing? Your body is talking to you, so pay attention to it. Here are things that might help:

- Try to name the feeling.
- Where in your body is the feeling?
- Breathe into that area of your body.
- Ask for help from a fellow student, faculty member, coach, or counselor.

How do you feel when you procrastinate? What do you do about it?

Also, you can listen to the CYH with a sympathetic ear. Does the fear sound like your five-year-old self who needs safety and reassurance? If so, pat her on the head and say to her, "Yes, this is scary. I am putting myself out there. Judgment will happen. I am an adult and I can handle this." Your fear tries to protect you. Acknowledge what it is telling you and move forward.

Maybe it is perfectionism. Do you try to work on your project and sit in front of the computer screen or a blank piece of paper and nothing happens? Does everything you write sound terrible? Your reaction is to delete it or wad up the paper to throw in the recycle bin. Wadding up a piece of paper is such a satisfying action, but, alas, impossible to perform with a computer.

Before graduate school, I didn't consider myself a perfectionist. Then I read an article where the author asked if readers avoided starting something new due to the fear that it wouldn't be done well (read "perfectly"). Busted! Damn. I learned it helps to name the perfectionist part of the CYH. Mine is called The Demon Perfectionist. If asked to draw a picture of her, she has wild electrified hair, big buggy eyes, sharp teeth, and she wails.

Whenever she raises her head and starts in on me saying, "You'll never get it right! Why are you even trying?" I try to be gentle with her as well as the other voices in my head. I realize they are trying to protect me. I ask the Demon what it is I'm afraid of. I try to reassure her. *Yes, what we are trying to do is scary, but I can handle it.*

 **Draw the perfectionist voice in your head and name it.**

Causes of writing fear. What's behind this fear thing? Yes, you could spend years in psychoanalysis figuring it out, but for now, let's look at the obvious. One fear is you will fail. Break down the fear of failure into two types. The first is you will put everything you have into this project and it will not be good enough for your faculty committee. The second is you won't be able to do it at all. The CYH imagines no matter how hard you try you won't finish it.

The direct opposite of these fears is you will succeed and everyone will think you are great. But the CYH reminds you: Deep down inside, you are a fraud. You don't believe you can do this and if you do, then there must be something wrong with the process that didn't weed you out.

Ouch! There is way too much pain in these paragraphs. Of course, absolutely none of it is true!

HOW TO SABOTAGE YOUR DISSERTATION

What do you do about the fears thrashing around in your head and keeping you up at night? The first step is recognizing the fear or at least considering that maybe fear might be what's going on. Try this experiment. Write down three things of which you might be afraid. Notice I've made this hypothetical because if you sneak around the CYH with hypothetical experiments, sometimes it doesn't notice what you are doing. Here I've given you examples:

- I'm afraid I'll fail.
- I'm afraid I'm not good enough.
- I'm afraid I'm a fraud.

 **What three things are you afraid of regarding your dissertation?**

Great. You've got something down on paper. Now look at those fears and decide how likely they are to be true. What safeguards can you create to protect you from the fears becoming real? For example, I'm afraid I'll fail. Break down what failure would look like. Then brainstorm what you could do to prevent these failure triggers from occurring. Understanding your fear is a great tool for dealing with it.

Your writing fear is real and it is not real. The CYH tells you that you can't do it and scolds you for even thinking you could. What do you do? You can control the volume of the CYH. When it starts harping on you, put your fingers in your ears and say, "La-la-la-la." I joke about fingers in your ears, but there are physical things you can do to handle fear. For instance:

- ✓ Use affirmations.
- ✓ Music can calm fears. Find music for writers on YouTube.
- ✓ Go for a walk until the fear subsides.
- ✓ Practice deep breathing and meditation.
- ✓ Incorporate tapping techniques. (Look it up on Google)

 **Which of these physical activities do you think would work for you? Are there others?**

You have to become aware of the CYH and not let it get to you. I know it sounds easy to do, and I assure you it is not, but start somewhere. I searched online for "affirmations for overcoming fear" and came up with 101 affirmations, for example: "I have nothing to be afraid of." Override the negative thoughts with positive thoughts: *I can do this. The department accepted me. They think I can do it. My advisor, who knows me best, thinks I can do it. I can do this.*

Consider Fay Focused-and-Quiet. She had a habit of telling herself she couldn't hack graduate school even though her undergraduate grades and GRE scores were well within the range expected for a

DEAR DISSERTATION WRITER

graduate student in our department. Her grades in her graduate classes were good, too. However, when it came time to write her dissertation, the CYH kept telling Fay she couldn't possibly do it.

When she told me she felt inadequate to write a dissertation, I asked Fay whether the CYH had anything positive to say about her abilities. Positives? Nope. I suggested (even if it felt silly) before she sat down to work on her dissertation, she look in the mirror and say out loud, "I can write a dissertation. My advisor thinks I can write this dissertation. Therefore, I will go write my dissertation." Over the next weeks, the CYH lessened its critical comments and Fay was able to write.

You don't have to handle fear on your own. Get help. Go online and get a list of books about writing fears or check out your university's writing center. Enlist the help of a friend or a group of friends with whom you can share. They may have the same feelings but are afraid to share them. Do you have an extremely obliging faculty member to help you over these humps? Hire a coach to help you recognize and deal with these fears. If you can't get over your anxiety on your own, check out your university's counseling center. You pay for this service through your university fees. Please use it.

Ursula Uncertain was an older-than-than-average doctoral student who was doing her graduate degree while working a full-time job at a law firm. When it was time for her to write her dissertation, she became afraid of what her advisor would say about her writing and could not bring herself to turn in the chapters she had written. The sad part of this story is Ursula didn't get over her fear even though after turning something in, her advisor generally gave her useful pointers on ways to improve her writing. Finally, because it had been so long since she had turned in a portion of her dissertation, the department ended her doctoral program.

Ursula's story is sad and true. Most students do not have this unhappy ending. I worked with Amy Get-It-Right, who was afraid she was doing a terrible job of writing her lit review. However, after reading it her faculty advisor made suggestions that allowed Amy to make revisions. We rehearsed affirmations to use when it was time to turn in a completed draft, such as, reminding herself that her writing got better every time her advisor read her work, which helped the anxiety of turning something in. She became less fearful each time she did her affirmation and turned something in.

 **What are your procrastinator or perfectionist tendencies?**

Dear Dissertation Writer,

Stewing in fear is not fun and it isn't getting your project finished. The symptoms and causes of fear, along with the actions you can take, are unique to you and universal to all students. Find an activity or outlet to reward yourself after writing. Enlist mentors to support you. Research or ask around to see what tools and techniques help others mute the CYH. Put your best effort into your draft and know the gift of your faculty advisor's feedback is coming. Accept your draft will mature and become stronger with each rewrite. Writing is messy, so allow yours to grow.

DEAR DISSERTATION WRITER

Whether you feel or feign the confidence at this very moment, write, turn it in, and rewrite.

Remember:
- ❏ Override negative thoughts with positive thoughts.
- ❏ Recognize what you are doing is scary and do it anyway.
- ❏ Get something written, then improve it.
- ❏ Get help:
    - ❏ Hire a writing coach.
    - ❏ Gather fellow graduate students for a writing session.
    - ❏ Schedule a session with a writing tutor in the university writing center.
    - ❏ See a counselor at your university's counseling center.

Chapter 3
THINK OF IT THIS WAY: IT'S NO BIG DEAL! IT'S LOTS OF SMALL DEALS!

Nothing is particularly hard if you divide it into smaller jobs.

~ Henry Ford

I started writing my dissertation more seriously when I realized it was no big deal and, therefore, I could do it. I remember the moment this thought occurred to me. I was on a three-mile power walk with my husband, which means we were walking for exercise, not fun. Either the oxygenated blood or the silence worked on my brain that day. My husband is not a talker giving me time to think.

Of course, I was stewing about my huge project, **THE DISSERTATION**. I had not been working on it, but it was never far from my thinking. I'd collected the data and analyzed it, but I wasn't writing. On the walk, I mulled over the construction of my dissertation. It would be an introduction, three data chapters, and a concluding chapter for five total chapters.

The introductory chapter is where I'd tell my reader about the theories used (the dreaded—to me— lit review), what I'd researched (rationale and research questions), and how I'd done the research (methods). I'd finish with a concluding chapter reviewing the theory, the methods, and the data and how they supported each other. I'd follow up with why the research was relevant and its limitations. Finally, I'd project future research projects based on my findings.

Between the introductory chapter and the concluding chapter, I'd have three data chapters. Then it hit me. Hadn't I recently finished taking three courses a semester for five semesters? Didn't I have to write a research paper in almost every class? In the last semester alone, I wrote three papers for my comprehensive exams. I'd written three-fifths of a dissertation every semester! And the dissertation should be an easier project because the chapters/papers were related to the same overarching topic and literature review. I could do this because I had already done it many times. I came home from the walk feeling exhilarated because suddenly, I knew I could write a dissertation.

It was no big deal!

THINK OF IT THIS WAY: IT'S NO BIG DEAL! IT'S LOTS OF SMALL DEALS!

I repeated the "It's no big deal!" mantra throughout the time I wrote my dissertation. Notice I didn't use this mantra as I was collecting and analyzing the data. Those are different mental processes entirely. The "no big deal" thinking was during the writing process.

 **How can you "no big deal" your dissertation?**

A dissertation is not the apex of your academic career. I was walking across campus on a beautiful spring day and saw Amy Do-It-Right sitting on a bench under a tree with a rather pensive look on her face. I called to her and when she waved me over, I joined her.

"Wow, this is a lovely spot. What's going on?" I said.

"I don't know if I can complete a project as large as this dissertation is," she said.

"It can feel like it's taking over your life. May I ask if you are planning to become an academic when you finish?"

"Yes, I am."

"Have you thought you might write a book someday? Possibly submit research papers from the dissertation."

"Yes, probably," she said.

"Try thinking of it this way. The dissertation is the biggest project you have done to date and I'm pretty sure you'll have bigger projects in the future. Does this framework help somewhat?"

"Yeah, I think it does. Thanks."

I've talked to graduate students who think the dissertation is the apex of their academic careers. Honestly, it is the biggest piece of writing a graduate student has ever done up to this point. Writing a dissertation is a short-term big deal. In the long scheme, looking at this project from the end of a scholastic life, this academic tome is the first of many big, long, and comprehensive pieces of writing to come. The writer in you is imagining research articles galore and, maybe, even a book or two. Hopefully, your dissertation will become a published work. A dissertation from this vantage point shows "it's no big deal!"

 **What future projects would you like to write that would make the dissertation look like "no big deal?"**

THINK OF IT THIS WAY: IT'S NO BIG DEAL! IT'S LOTS OF SMALL DEALS!

Dear Dissertation Writer,

Stare your dissertation monster in the eye and repeat after me: "It's no big deal!"

Remember:

- ❏ You have created smaller versions of a dissertation already in course research papers.
- ❏ You will create bigger projects than your dissertation in an academic career.
- ❏ It's no big deal!

Chapter 4
BRAVE SAVES THE DAY

Vulnerability is the birthplace of innovation, creativity, and change.

~ **Brené Brown**

I returned from lunch to find Steve Social-Star leaning against the wall near my office door. "Would you like to come in?" I said as I unlocked the door.

When he agreed, I said, "What's up with the long face?"

"Well, I have an idea and it scares the crap out of me."

"Tell me more."

"It's really a cool idea, but it is way out in left field," he said. "I'm afraid my advisor is going to think I'm a nut case."

He proceeded to explain his idea and how it was based on the data he'd gathered.

"I can see why an idea might make you feel vulnerable," I said. "On the other hand, I'd hate for this idea to not see the light of day due to fear of ridicule."

"I'll think more about it," he said as he left. "I'd hate to lose it, too. Thanks for letting me thrash it out here."

When Brené Brown wrote the book *Daring Greatly*, she was a research professor at the University of Houston's Graduate College of Social Work. In her research, she discovered that people who refuse to be vulnerable shut down creatively. She noted a person's willingness to be vulnerable is the crux of creativity. Not being willing to risk putting new ideas out to the world for fear of being attacked, crushes creativity.

 **In what ways do you or have you shut down your creativity?**

What does vulnerability have to do with writing a dissertation?
A dissertation is research resulting in previously unknown findings. The presentation of the research to your advisor, then your committee, and eventually to the academic world is an act of being vulnerable. The presentation of what you have discovered to all of those who may, or may not, agree with your findings is an act of vulnerability.

Researchers do shake up the scientific world with their findings. I want to share two stories of researchers who presented results that were contrary to established beliefs. Imagine the emotional difficulty of going against established paradigms with the sure knowledge the data supported your findings despite other researchers' disdain.

Geologists received the notion of plate tectonics poorly when Alfred Wegener supported it in his 1915 book, *The Origin of Continents and Oceans*. Other geologists were confident that continents did not drift and thought Wegener a fool. His support for new ideas went against established thinking. Did he give up? No! He continued putting himself on the

DEAR DISSERTATION WRITER

edge of risk, dying fifteen years later on an expedition in Greenland. The theory of plate tectonics is now an established geological fact, along with Wegener's place as the founder of a significant scientific theory. His willingness to support an unpopular theory, despite being vulnerable to the attacks thrown his way, benefited science in the end.

When Barry Marshall presented the notion bacteria caused most peptic ulcers, the medical community lambasted the idea partly because no animal trials could prove it. To show the truth of his claim, Barry Marshall drank an *H. pylori* solution, the bacteria he thought caused ulcers, and developed an ulcer.

Yuck! Talk about believing in the power of vulnerability. Marshall was willing to develop a peptic ulcer to show the world his unorthodox theory was correct. Marshall, an Australian physician, and his long-time collaborator, pathologist Robin Warren, won the 2005 Nobel Prize in Medicine for their research. New ideas do not always conform to established knowledge.

I don't expect your dissertation research will shake up the established paradigms of a field. However, your research will be claiming new findings. Be prepared for possible pushback.

The CYH may start asking difficult and scary questions, which uncovers the vulnerability of presenting original research.

- *What if I'm wrong?*
- *What if someone exposes me?*
- *What if someone attacks my findings and me?*

Being brave requires being vulnerable and not allowing critics to silence you, even internal critics. Vulnerability may feel like you are opening up your heart for someone to put a knife in it. Perhaps everyone will love the new ideas. Wouldn't that be wonderful? However, be aware there may be researchers who do not agree with your findings. Be sure to present them as clearly as possible with the best supporting evidence.

While working on my master's degree, I met a fellow graduate student Leslie Jarmon who was a couple of years ahead of me. When she wrote her dissertation, she knew her topic was outside the accepted theories in her chosen field of Conversation Analysis. Her claim that nonverbal cues often substituted for a verbal answer as a turn in a conversation was a first in this field. Leslie believed she had more to gain than to lose, but she needed evidence. She used video-recorded conversations to prove her assertion and showed her committee examples of the behavior. Previous to her use of video, most Conversation Analysis researchers had used audio recordings and had not seen the evidence that Leslie provided. Her claims were difficult to refute given the evidence she amassed. On top of having unconventional claims, she arranged with the University of Texas Graduate School to submit her dissertation on a DVD, which had not been done before. Leslie expected that seeing the evidence would be far more persuasive than merely describing the behaviors of her observed subjects.

Anticipate how critics could potentially attack your idea. Leslie knew her critics might not accept her assertions without video proof, so she used visual evidence. What actions early in the process of formulating claims or gathering data can you take to allay possible critiques? Anticipate the questions and have answers.

Beyond doing the best research you can, don't take responsibility for the reactions of others. As long as you do your job to the fullest, trust. The rest is out of your hands.

However, listen carefully to your critics. Decide if they have constructive suggestions that make this new idea better. Not all criticism is wrong.

 **How much and what kind of data do you need to collect to prove your claims?**

Fear of being attacked for new ideas. In Chapter 2, I wrote about fear stalling dissertation writing. Fear of being attacked can be added to the list of fears. Handle it precisely the way it was discussed earlier. Once the new finding based on data appears clear to you, discuss it with your faculty advisor. Hopefully, the relationship is a good one and you will not mind being vulnerable in presenting the new finding. Once your faculty advisor is convinced, your dissertation committee will be next.

 **When have you been vulnerable with your advisor? How did it go?**

On the other side of this concept, when you are in a position to criticize, be a kind critic when hearing new ideas that go against the established norm especially if you choose to join academia as a faculty member. New claims in student research should be common. Think carefully about the evidence and consider accepting the idea before trashing it. Who knows? It might be the beginning of an amazing finding. Of course, it may be lunatic ravings, too, but be kind in criticizing it. Be open to the possibility that conventional thought may be incorrect.

Dear Dissertation Writer,

Stand tall. Be vulnerable and create.

Remember:

❏ Feeling vulnerable or unsafe shuts down creativity.

❏ New ideas are not always immediately accepted by peers.

❏ Fear of sharing new ideas with your advisor and committee may stall dissertation writing.

Chapter 5
HOW TO LOSE CONTROL

Grant me the serenity to accept the things I can't change,
Courage to change the things I can,
And wisdom to know the difference.

~ Reinhold Niebuhr, AA 12-Steps Program

Steve Social-Star came to my office one afternoon, fuming, "My advisor hasn't given me the revisions on my chapter yet. I need it so I can get back to working on it. I need it now!"

"Is this a longer amount of time than he usually takes?" I said.

"No, not really, but it drives me crazy not to get it back for a week."

We talked about what he could do while he waited for his advisor to return a draft. Here are thoughts we came up with:

- ✓ Have a conversation with your faculty advisor early in the dissertation process about normal turn-around times for revisions.
- ✓ Be working on more than one part of the dissertation. This enables writing to continue while the faculty advisor has a different part. For example, when a section, such as the literature review, is in your faculty advisor's hands, be working on the beginning of the methodology section. By having a different part to work on, no writing time is wasted while your faculty advisor reads your work.
- ✓ If your faculty advisor takes an unusually long time to return a draft, send a polite email saying "I have not heard back regarding the chapter I sent on [state the date]. Let me know if you have questions about it."

What you can't control. The biggest thing out of your control is your faculty advisor. You don't know what his professional challenges are or what is going on in his life personally. Nor what health crises he may face. These things will influence how quickly he provides his revisions.

Little will annoy faculty advisors more than a student taking months to turn in a draft and then, expecting a response in three days. It is a big faculty advisor-advisee "no-no" to complain about the time it has taken to return a revision. If you want quick turn-arounds, practice quick turn-ins.

Another uncontrollable factor is whether your advisor will approve of the writing. Strategies under "advisor control" could be:

- Early planning with your faculty advisor
- Using pre-writing strategies with your faculty advisor, such as brainstorming, outlining, identifying primary and secondary resources
- Checking in regularly to review strategy
- Preparing early drafts and quick turn-around on your part

Moving from personal to technical, you can't control computer crashes or theft. We'll discuss more about computer "control" in the next section. Hard drives are mechanical; they can and will fail. This fact of life doesn't have to mean lost data. While we are talking about mechanical failures, you have no control over car or household appliances continuing to work. These kinds of failures can eat up valuable writing time.

Other things you can't control:

- Health (your own or others)
- The weather
- The person driving a car on the same street

When everything uncontrollable is spelled out in black and white, it is enough to keep you from ever getting out of bed. See where the first line of the serenity quote comes into play? Know there are uncontrollable happenings. Accept it and get out of bed with the thought that whatever comes along, you will deal with it.

What is within your control? The second line of the quote says courage is needed to deal with the things in your control such as a schedule for collecting data and writing. Curt Competent wrote at his best first thing in the morning. He got up, showered, made coffee, sat at

HOW TO LOSE CONTROL

his desk, and wrote for an hour or two.

Fay Focused-and-Quiet wrote best after midnight. She worked on the school's computers in the graduate student lounge when it was empty. I thought she was crazy, but who am I to judge? She finished her dissertation writing in this way.

Even though you can't control a computer hard drive crashing, you can control keeping the computer virus-finding programs and the operating system updated. You are in control of not taking a laptop to the coffee shop and leaving it on the table while you take a restroom break. Coming back to find it missing is heartbreaking and well within your control. You are in control of not putting a laptop on top of an unstable pile of papers with the power cord draped across the walkway. These may sound like outlandish examples, but they did happen. Finally, back up everything written. Either put it in Google Docs or on a flash drive every time something is changed. Taking these kinds of precautions makes what can't be controlled a lot more palatable.

Even though you can't control if illness strikes, what is in your control is getting enough exercise and sleep, and eating well. I know the stereotypical grad student lives on fast food, short nights, and lots of alcohol. I am quite sure those students are much less likely to finish grad school.

 **How are you caring for your health?**

DEAR DISSERTATION WRITER

Quality of writing is under your control. If writing is a problem, go to the university's writing center and ask for help. Hire an editor to clean up grammar. Remember editing doesn't happen without writing. Write and improve it later.

With help, control the anxiety experienced concerning the uncontrollable. If debilitating anxiety prevails, most universities have a counseling center with experienced counselors. Please take advantage of those services. Sharing your feelings with a loved one or a fellow graduate student can also help. They may have had similar problems. Writing is a solitary activity, be sure and plan social outings with friends to refresh and relax. Going into nature is a good idea. Take a walk in a park, breathe clean air, and listen to the birds sing.

 **How are you dealing with your anxiety?**

HOW TO LOSE CONTROL

Know the difference. The poem's final line asks for help in discerning the difference between the controllable things and those that are uncontrollable. This is no small feat. For example, weather falls under uncontrollable. Is staying in an option? You control staying at home during inclement weather or writing at the library or a coffee shop where the temperature on a sweltering day is controlled. Bundle up or wear fewer clothes depending on the weather. Within the broader framework of things you can't control, what are the things over which you have a measure of control?

What are the academic things falling into the uncontrollable category? Think about how you can exercise a modicum of control within the larger uncontrollable things. For example, since your advisor's schedule falls into uncontrollable, discuss with her what her usual turn-around policy is and request if there is going to be a change, she'll send an email.

As discussed earlier, computer hard drive crashes taking unfinished work with it fall into the uncontrollable category. However, backing up the work by putting it in the cloud or on a flash drive is within your ability to control. Backing up is a good habit and guards against uncontrollable happenings. This is the wisdom of knowing the difference between things you can control and things you can't.

 **Where do you backup your dissertation data and writing?**

DEAR DISSERTATION WRITER

Dear Dissertation Writer,

Don't let the uncontrollable be paralyzing. Recognize what you can't control and what you can control. Figure out a strategy to deal with the things you can control, accept the things you can't, and continue to write. Whoo-hoo! I hear the keys clacking now!

Remember:

❏ You can control your attitude toward writing.

❏ You can talk to your advisor about a schedule for receiving feedback.

❏ You can control backing up your work.

Section 2: TOPICS, PROPOSALS, COMMITTEES, ... OH MY!

Chapter 6
TOPIC? SCHMOPIC? DECIDE ALREADY!

In much of society, research means to investigate something you do not know or understand.

~ Neil Armstrong

Do not follow where the path may lead. Go, instead, where there is no path and leave a trail.

~ Ralph Waldo Emerson

Ursula Uncertain dropped by my office and asked if I had time to talk.

"Sure," I said. "What's up?"

"I can't come up with a decent topic for my dissertation," she said.

"Well, that can be a challenge sometimes."

This story may bring up gnashing of teeth and the supersonic wails of psychic angst from readers' CYH. You understand Ursula's problem. How do you choose what to research? Picking a topic with meat on it; that is, a topic with real unknowns to find something new can be a challenge. Also don't pick too big a topic either. The nitty-gritty of dissertation writing is about picking a topic and deciding how to research it.

TOPIC? SCHMOPIC? DECIDE ALREADY!

If you have taken a research methods course or two and conducted real research in those courses, then the following is a review. The rationale reads, "Based on Jones and Smith's Theory of Something Relevant, I have noticed a lack of research in this particular area which is critical to a full understanding of this phenomenon." Followed by, "The question I am asking is, 'How often this phenomenon occurs within a population of freshman college students?'" Or, the question might be, "What does it look like?" The question's form will determine the methodology. When a research question asks how many or how often, then it leads to quantitative analysis. When it asks what does it look like, then it will be a qualitative study.

What does your faculty advisor research? Curt Competent had a faculty advisor who was very high profile in his research area. Curt understood the legacy his faculty advisor had from his long-ago advisor, so he included this legacy when he wrote out his dissertation topic. The discussion with his faculty advisor about the topic and his long-ago advisor went well. His faculty advisor was pleased with the proposal and suggested several papers they might co-author from the dissertation's results. That's a win!

Remember a faculty advisor spends considerable time discussing, reading, and suggesting revisions on a student's dissertation. For this reason, some faculty advisors feel the research the student has done is partly their own, hence the offer to co-author papers based on the student's research. In general, co-authoring a paper with a big name in a field is good for a student's reputation regardless of who did the bulk of the research.

Pay attention to what Curt Competent did with his advisor. Curt:

- ✓ Recognized the legacy his faculty advisor had with his long-ago advisor.
- ✓ Chose a topic within this legacy.
- ✓ Agreed to co-author papers from his research with his faculty advisor.

Amy Get-It-Right had not had this kind of conversation with her faculty advisor. After she graduated, she received an offer to publish her dissertation as an academic book. During the publishing process, her faculty advisor made it known to Amy she expected recognition as co-author of the book. Amy was surprised and upset about this revelation. However, to keep the peace and with the understanding that her faculty advisor had helped a lot with the final shape of the dissertation, she agreed to the co-author arrangement.

Pick a topic or theory you like. If your department allows students to choose their topics, read on. If not, skip this chapter. Otherwise, pick a topic of interest to you, one that is extremely interesting, because by the time you've finished with the dissertation, it will be much less attractive. Ambivalence about the topic at the start can lead to strong distaste, even hatred of it by the time the dissertation is finished. Think about how much harder it will be to write about an unloved topic from the start. If at all possible, don't do that.

A topic should start with what the theory predicts, but has not yet been proven, often called a gap in the theory. Write what is called the rationale to explain what theory you are using and why your topic or question is important to this theory.

 **On what theory or theories are you basing your research?**

TOPIC? SCHMOPIC? DECIDE ALREADY!

Is the topic the right scope? Is your topic too broad or too narrow? How to know? Your faculty advisor is a good source for this information. When I revealed to the reader of my master's thesis the topic my faculty advisor and I had chosen, she told me the questions I asked would fill two dissertations. It was certainly too big for a master's thesis. I responded, no, I wasn't expecting to find all of the phenomena mentioned, but they were possibilities. She was somewhat mollified by my answer.

Is your topic too broad? Here are questions to help you to pare it down:

- *How long will data gathering take? Less time is better.*
- *If too long, how do you pare the topic down?*
- *How many questions are you asking? Will fewer questions work?*
- *Can the questions be more specific?*
- *Do you know whether your topic has a manageable scope?*

Another question to ask before committing to a topic is, "Has this topic already been asked, researched, and published?" If so, what new knowledge will your research add to the world? If it is not new, what could make it something new? Does the previous research need to be run with a control or be done with a different population? Those two changes could add to academic knowledge.

 **What is (are) your research question(s)?**

DEAR DISSERTATION WRITER

Where do you find a topic? In my program, I took fifteen classes. In some of them, I wrote research papers for which I collected real data. Is expanding one of your class papers possible? The nice part about using a previous paper is you already have the start of a literature review, as well as a fleshed-out methodology.

You may have already taken a paper from a class and expanded it to present at a conference. This is an even better start because there is likely more data for a conference paper than a class paper. It is possible after the presentation, a respondent gave feedback on the paper with ideas about how to expand the research or its limitations. Don't discount the limitations. They are valuable in writing a dissertation because the limitations must be addressed in the last chapter of the dissertation. Your committee wants to know you realize every question hasn't been answered fully and no research is perfect.

Other dissertations on similar topics can be useful in finding a topic as well, especially dissertations by students who worked with the same faculty advisor. Look at the limitations in the last chapter of their finished dissertation for questions remaining about the topic. Do any of them catch your interest?

Perhaps your faculty advisor has a topic she wants to have researched or owns data she wants to be mined. It is not cheating to get suggestions from others. They have many ideas and are not able to give their time to them all.

Maybe they intuit a particular topic that would fit your research style. Don't be afraid to use that feeling and then think about the topics suggested.

Fay Focused-and-Quiet was at a loss for a research topic. She worked with a faculty member who had a big research project and was happy to share the data. Luckily, they were able to add a questionnaire into the subject pool for Fay to use. The union made both parties happy. Take it if they offer you an interesting one!

Another possibility may be to research a theory wildly new if you find it interesting. Yes, this is a stretch for a graduate student or a faculty member for that matter. Doing this will require reading about the theories behind the idea and the best methods to research it, which will likely create a lot of in-depth research before figuring out where to begin. It might add months to your process. However, extreme excitement about a topic is never a bad idea.

One last possible problem with selecting a topic. What if there are many fantastic research topics in mind and you are having trouble narrowing it down to one? Consider choosing the topic easiest to research. Or, choose a topic by justifying using a certain group of people (such as undergraduate students) as subjects. If you have done a lot of work on a theory, perhaps focus on a unique angle within the theory. A dissertation is a lot of work; make it as easy on yourself as possible.

How do you know if your topic is viable? Have a conceptual conversation with a partner, preferably your faculty advisor, but maybe not. Someone outside your field might be a good choice because she will ask questions about assumptions, while someone in the field might share those assumptions and may not think to ask about them.

A dissertation coach could be helpful, especially someone who has an academic background. Be assured such a coach knows the questions needing to be answered and will ask those questions. Yes, that is a shameless plug, but also good advice.

 **Where do you think is the best place to look for a topic?**

Think about the subjects needed with the chosen topic. You have a topic and have discussed it with someone outside your brain. What subjects are needed? In a humanities field, such as psychology, anthropology, or communication, this is a real issue. When studying microbes, it is not. Bacteria don't get a say in whether or not they want to participate in a study.

Paul Planner was a married graduate student with two children. For his family's sake, he wanted to get his doctorate as quickly as possible. He thought if he used college freshmen as his subjects, he would be able to find participants for his study because most universities have lots of freshmen. Even better, he worked for residential life and had ample opportunity to recruit subjects. He crafted his question so that university freshmen were the perfect research subjects.

Steve Social-Star told his committee he wanted to study the coping skills of people in difficult times. His academic committee told him he should use people who had lost their jobs. Sounds easy to find those subjects, doesn't it? Nope. As it turned out, most people who had lost their jobs were not interested in helping a researcher. He spent at least eighteen months gathering data until he had enough to do a decent analysis. He got it done, but it was a long slog from prospective defense to dissertation defense. Always keep in mind the difficulty of finding participants when crafting your topic question.

What population do you have in mind? It should be relevant to the questions asked. If you want to study the end of life, there won't be a lot of subjects in a pool of college students. Be specific about the population. When studying how siblings interact, determine what age siblings to study. Be specific about demographics.

TOPIC? SCHMOPIC? DECIDE ALREADY!

 **Who are your participants?**

What methods are needed to research this population? Be sure to take methods courses and do practice research papers to be comfortable with different methods of research. Beware of picking a research method first. A professor warned students, "If you have a hammer, notice everything starts looking like a nail." In other words, even if you like doing a specific type of research method, not every research question will be best answered by the favored method. Remember, when asking how much or how many, that's a quantitative method, like a survey. If you are asking, "What does it look like?" the answer requires a qualitative method, such as grounded theory, ethnography, focus groups, or interviews.

 **What is your methodology?**

Why is this research question important? I know it is hard to believe, but not every research question is worth researching. Convince yourself first, and then your faculty advisor of the importance of researching this unknown. If the argument isn't convincing to yourself or your faculty advisor, how will it possibly sway your dissertation committee? Spend time figuring out why others would care about this question. It is the rationale.

TOPIC? SCHMOPIC? DECIDE ALREADY!

 **What is your answer to the "who cares" question? This is the rationale.**

Picking a dissertation topic both you and your faculty advisor like is the absolute first step to take. I met students who knew what they wanted to research when they applied to graduate school. However, beware of holding on to a topic too tightly. Something fascinating might come up later in your coursework. On the other end of the continuum are the students who have no idea what to research.

Dear Dissertation Writer,

Wherever you land on the continuum of picking a topic, you have to pick one. Get to thinking!

Remember:

❏ Think about faculty legacy.

❏ Pick a topic/theory you like.

❏ Use a class research paper topic or a conference presentation.

❏ Ask your faculty advisor for suggestions.

❏ Go with a whole new idea.

❏ How difficult will it be to find subjects for this research?

❏ Think about methodology also.

Chapter 7
YEP, YOUR FATE IS IN THEIR HANDS

Actors are a lot like professors on dissertation committees - it's a lot of ego, a lot of rallying for position, there is a lot at stake in every single interaction.

~ **Mayim Bialic**

Amy Get-it-Right sent me an email with a subject line reading: "Help! I have to form a dissertation committee." She discovered putting together a dissertation committee was an extremely daunting task for her. I suggested she come to my office and we could talk through strategies.

Even if your dissertation committee is easy to form, read on as I have suggestions I hope will be helpful. Who you choose to be on your committee is an important decision because these are the people who help you write your dissertation. In the end, they hold your academic fate in their hands.

Who should they be? The first and foremost reason to ask a faculty member to be on your dissertation committee is their research is related to your topic or methodology. Asking a physics professor to serve on a sociology dissertation committee makes no sense. Ideally, ask faculty members with whom you have a relationship.

Often graduate schools suggest and sometimes require, graduate students take coursework in affiliated areas. This requirement is to force students to meet faculty members outside their department who might be helpful on their committees. I studied Interpersonal Communication and took coursework in social linguistics, social psychology, educational psychology, and anthropology. All of these departments study interpersonal communication with a different slant than the faculty in my department. It was helpful to learn how things are different across the academy. Further, I met accomplished and interesting faculty in these courses. Do the same. Take coursework outside the department and meet those faculty members.

YEP, YOUR FATE IS IN THEIR HANDS

 **Who will be on your committee?**

How many members? When forming a dissertation committee, know what your graduate school's requirements are for committee members. The university where I worked required five to six members and one to two of them from outside the department. Check with your departmental graduate coordinator or graduate administrator to confirm what the rules are for your degree.

Yes, asking your faculty advisor how many people need to be on your committee is an option, and he might have the correct answer. However, faculty advisors do not grant degrees. Go to the source, the graduate school, or a graduate school representative, to be sure to get the right answer. This information should be on the graduate school's website. I find seeing it in writing is soothing. Having a committee incorrectly set up is not a snag you want to have on the way to earning your degree. Be certain!

Curt Competent invited six faculty members to be on his committee, which was more than he needed.

I thought six was excessive because another person on the committee is a possible dissenter that wasn't required. "Are you sure you want six members? You need only five," I asked him.

"I've got a complicated dissertation and I want outside opinions on it," he said. It worked for him.

Should personality make a difference? Let's talk about the personalities of the people on your committee. Hopefully, you have taken classes with them. Did you enjoy working with this person? If he was a misogynist blowhard in class, why would he be different on your committee? Don't ask him. If she was critical of everything in class, again she isn't likely to be different on your committee. Don't ask her.

But what if she is the expert in your area of interest? That's a hard one. Is this faculty member's quirk worth tolerating? Think about changing your topic slightly, eliminating the need for a difficult person. Invite people with whom you've had pleasant interactions and who believe in the project.

Do these people need to like and/or respect each other? Once you have ideas about who you'd like to have on your committee. Think about how these people get along with each other. Do Dr. Joe Blow and Dr. Suzy Splendid see eye-to-eye on the value of the chosen methodology or another piece of your dissertation?

Steve Social-Star had an inside member of his committee, Dr. Joe Blow, who thought the outside member's methodology was not valid. Dr. Blow and Dr. Splendid spent half of Steve's meeting arguing with each

YEP, YOUR FATE IS IN THEIR HANDS

other over methodology and it wasn't even in his dissertation. His dissertation was approved, but his defense was a stressful affair, which could have been avoided.

On the othe hand, Paul Planner's committee members were friends and respected each other's research. His dissertation defense was more like a party. That's how you want yours to be.

How do I know if my committee members get along? Use your university contacts. What do fellow graduate students think? Have they heard rumors of clashes between these faculty members? Ask the friendly graduate administrators in your departmental office. Don't hesitate to ask your faculty advisor this specific question. They might not think of interpersonal conflicts between your committee members if not asked. Once asked, I am sure your advisor will tell you perhaps Dr. Joe Blow and Dr. Suzy Splendid might not be the best combination for this committee.

If Steve Social-Star had asked me in my capacity as graduate coordinator for my opinion of the people he planned to ask to serve on his committee, I would have suggested he not put those two in the same room. Yes, they were both excellent researchers, but they simply didn't agree on methodology. It's fine and good for the academy to have differing points of view on research. Not good during your dissertation defense. Ask only one of them.

 **Ask fellow graduate students and your faculty advisor what they think about your planned combination of faculty members. Their answers:**

What if I can't get anyone I know on my committee? There may be no faculty member who would best fit the topic you have chosen. Once again, rely on your faculty advisor to suggest someone; hopefully, even several people. Asking peers if they have worked with these unknown faculty members can help. Before contacting these recommended people, read their CVs. Most faculty members post theirs online. Also, read the research published by these individuals.

If it is challenging to contact strangers and ask them to do a favor, remember that outside committee membership is a job responsibility for most faculty members. They may not mind being asked at all. If one of them says no, please know their refusal is not personal and is usually due to a faculty member's schedule. It is not a personal rejection! They don't know you well enough to reject you.

YEP, YOUR FATE IS IN THEIR HANDS

What if I want someone on my committee who isn't a faculty member at a university? There are usually procedures for this kind of committee member. Check with the graduate school to find out what the procedures are and follow them to the letter. Do not let an administrative screw-up derail the dissertation defense.

 Are there members who are outside your university or not traditional faculty members? What are the rules at your university?

Dear Dissertation Writer,

The short answer to the question of who should be on your committee is: Ask people you know and like who have expertise in your topic and methods. Be sure they get along with each other.

Go do it!

Remember:

- ❏ How many members of a dissertation committee does your graduate school require?
- ❏ If you can't find anyone you know, ask your faculty advisor and fellow graduate students for suggestions.
- ❏ If you want to ask someone who is not a faculty member at your university, check with your graduate school for their procedures.

Chapter 8
WHO'S ON FIRST? OR WHAT TO DO FIRST?

Organizing is what you do before you do something, so that when you do it, it is not all mixed up.

~ Winnie-the-Poo by A.A. Milne

Mary Military bounced into my office and sat down in the guest chair with a smile on her face. "Well, what's up?" I asked.

"I just came from my faculty advisor's office and he approved my topic and the committee members I chose. What's next?" she said.

I knew she was kidding me. She knew exactly what she needed to do next. She now needed a written proposal to show her committee what she planned to research for her dissertation based on what theory, why she thought this topic was important to research (rationale), how she planned to do the research (methods), and who her subjects would be. Along the way, she'd need to formally ask those committee members to serve on her committee. Finally, she'd need to have her proposal approved by her faculty advisor and then her committee at a proposal defense meeting.

Be sure to check for graduate school requirements. As I've said, again and again, check with your faculty advisor, graduate administrator, and/or graduate school for what is required for a proposal. Some students don't even have to write a proposal, because some departments do not require one. Know the rules of your school/department.

 **What are the rules at your university/department for proposals?**

WHO'S ON FIRST? OR WHAT TO DO FIRST?

I highly recommend creating a proposal and a proposal defense meeting with your committee, whether required or not. While it is scary to have your ideas discussed by faculty members, it would be scarier if the committee's first exposure to your ideas was after you spent months collecting data, analyzing the results, coming to conclusions, and writing it up.

In the department where I received my degree, the proposal meeting was a low-key discussion of ideas and research methods with the student's chosen group of experienced faculty members. Proposal meetings don't usually turn out to be the grilling that sometimes happens at a final dissertation defense.

Curt Competent's faculty advisor told him, "How often in your academic career does the opportunity come along to have a small group of highly respected researchers discussing your research ideas and offering suggestions before you do the work?" Not very often. Take advantage of the opportunity to listen to them and take notes on what sounds like good advice. Also, remember that some of what they say, you must do and are not just suggestions.

What goes in a proposal? A proposal should have an introduction with language in the future tense; that is, this is the research you propose to do, hence the name proposal. Next is a literature review introducing the theories upon which you are basing your research. The literature review can be in past tense because earlier research has been done and you are reporting how it relates to your research idea.

Somewhere in the introduction or literature review, tell your reader why your research question is worth researching, aka the rationale. Explain where the unknowns are in the research that this literature review has revealed and how the current research proposes to fill those gaps.

A methodology section explains how the proposed research will be done. What methods will be best for this research question? Will it need quantitative research methods, qualitative research methods, or a mixed-methods schema? Hopefully, you and your faculty advisor have thrashed out answers to those questions already.

A faculty advisor may want you to run a pilot study to discover if the proposed research is worth studying as well as possibly catching unexpected problems with the proposed methods. The pilot data and discussion will likely be a chapter of the proposal.

The proposal may be long or short. If you write all of the above, it might be the entire front half of your dissertation or if not, it may be a short twenty-page proposal. The length depends on the culture of the particular department or sub-area of research and maybe even your faculty advisor.

Ursula Uncertain was doing quantitative research in Interpersonal Communication and her proposal included the entire literature review, rationale, and methodology of her completed dissertation, which was nice. When it came time to write up the final dissertation, she had to write about only the data, the results, and the conclusion.

Fay Focused-and-Quiet was a rhetoric student in Communication Studies whose faculty advisor required less writing upfront. She wrote a short literature review saying what theories and theorists she planned to discuss in her dissertation and the subject matter she planned to analyze using these theories. A proposal like this sounds good during the proposal writing stage, but less pleasant during the final dissertation write-up when you have to do the in-depth literature discussion and how it applies to your subject. Both types of students end up doing the same amount of writing, just at different times of their dissertation writing.

 **What are the specific sections you need to have for YOUR proposal?**

WHO'S ON FIRST? OR WHAT TO DO FIRST?

Set up a proposal meeting. If you have a dissertation committee set up and your written proposal approved by your faculty advisor, meaning the proposal is ready to be evaluated by the dissertation committee, the next step is to set up a meeting where and when most of the committee can attend. By email, offer dates and times you are available or use whatever calendaring apps are currently popular. In the department where I studied and worked, we suggested giving students' committee members at least two weeks to read the document. The odds are good they won't read it until the day before, but don't assume anything.

 **In your department what is the suggested time between giving the committee a copy of the proposal and the date of the meeting?**

Further, give each of your committee members a copy of the proposal, either printed or electronic, before the two-week clock begins. Here again, each school or faculty member will have a preferred method of reading submissions. Find out what their preferences are. Do it the way they prefer. Why start with committee members reading your document annoyed with you because their preferences weren't followed?

 **How does each committee member want to have their copy of a proposal submitted to them?**

WHO'S ON FIRST? OR WHAT TO DO FIRST?

Be open to changes. When the day of your proposal defense arrives, take a deep breath and remember this is simply a proposal. Committee members will likely want changes to it. There may be places where you decide to take a firm stand on how to do this research. If so, have good theoretical reasons for not taking their suggestions and be prepared to defend them.

In general, it is likely to go better in the long run if you do what your dissertation committee suggests. I know they may ask more than you had planned. It happened to me. Nevertheless, this committee's approval is the final hurdle to your graduation. Keep the members happy.

For example, a friend of mine was studying parental favoritism and the communication between family members. She had planned for the family to be together when they filled out the questionnaires because the committee wanted the time frame reference for each family member to be the same. Her committee also wanted her to be present at each of these gatherings. She asked for a compromise because being at every data gathering would require extensive travel and expense. They agreed she could be on the telephone with them when they gathered to fill out the questionnaires, in case there were questions or problems. It was more work on her part, but it made her committee members happy. She did it their way.

Dear Dissertation Writer,

Congratulations on having a proposal written and ready to defend. Breathe and have a productive meeting.

Remember:

- ❏ Check for your university/department's proposal requirements.
- ❏ Proposal: Lit review, rationale, methodology, and maybe a pilot study.
- ❏ The proposal may be long or short.
- ❏ Set up a meeting.
- ❏ Be open to changes.

Chapter 9
WHAT'S IT SUPPOSED TO LOOK LIKE?

Three Rules of Work: Out of clutter find simplicity; From discord find harmony; In the middle of difficulty lies opportunity.

~ Albert Einstein

Paul Planner called me and said, "I'm working on my dissertation and trying to write the introduction, but I don't know what to say."

"Maybe the introduction isn't the best place to start writing a dissertation. I know it is the first section a person reads, but maybe not the best place to start writing," I said.

Every school has different format requirements for a dissertation. Find the person or the website page that explains your graduate school's rules. For example, some engineering schools require a dissertation include three papers published in peer-reviewed journals with supporting writings around the articles to put them in context. Students in such a department hopefully know this information early in their program and begin the work of getting research papers published as soon as possible.

 **What dissertation format does your graduate school require?**

WHAT'S IT SUPPOSED TO LOOK LIKE?

Structure of a dissertation. Are all dissertations in your department required to have the same structure? Congratulations, that's clear now. Even if they are not the same, completed dissertations of your advisor's former students will give a clue about the structure your faculty advisor is expecting.

My dissertation was a discourse analysis of the conversations of three different couples preparing and eating dinner captured on video recordings. I wrote about how the recorded conversations supported relationship maintenance. The format was an introductory chapter, which contained the literature review, rationale, and methodology. Other types of dissertations use two chapters; that is the literature review and rationale, and then, a separate chapter for methods. What determines the structure? It depends on how long the above-mentioned components are and whether a reader may want to head straight for them. It also depends on what your faculty advisor expects or thinks works best for this project.

Then my dissertation had three data chapters—three things I noticed supported relationship maintenance in the conversations of the couples I recorded. The first chapter analyzed catching up on what happened in the day; the next chapter looked at how the couples talked about friends and family; and, the final chapter examined how they talked about the future. I had an extensive discussion about each of the phenomena, examples to support the arguments, and discussions about the examples. Finally, I had a concluding chapter including a summary, an answer to the "why should anyone care" question (the rationale), limitations of the current research, and projections of future research possibilities.

Early in the process think about how you want to structure this dissertation and present it to your faculty advisor. After this discussion, she may have suggestions for changes. Remember this is the time for give-and-take with your faculty advisor. Digging in your heels about parts of it requires having sound theoretical or methodological reasons for not wanting to change something. Saying to any faculty advisor it would be more expedient to do it an easier way is a big mistake. There is nothing wrong with the "it's easier" motive. However, if it is wrapped up in a theoretical or a methodological reason, a desire to do it the easier way will be much more palatable for your faculty advisor to accept.

 **How will you structure your dissertation?**

Tell me three times. I used to teach public speaking. The mantra for presenting a speech was, "Tell them what you are going to tell them, then tell them. Finally, tell them what you told them." The same is true for a dissertation. The document will start with an introduction in which you tell the reader what you will be telling them in the next chapters. In the body of the speech and the internal chapters of the dissertation, tell the audience in detail what was described in the introduction. Finally in the conclusion, summarize what you told them in the internal chapters. The conclusion is the explanation of what you want them to understand from the research presented and what other research is possible in the future. This is how I structured my dissertation. Always follow your faculty advisor's lead in the structure of your dissertation.

In each of the three ways, the focus on the information is showcased differently. The introduction is an abbreviated telling to get the reader interested. The body is where the writer convinces the reader of the data's accuracy and interpretation with this dazzling research. Finally, the conclusion helps the reader understand how you went from Point A in the argument to Point B, along with helpful insights you realized during the research.

Don't write the introduction first. Just because the document starts with an introduction does not mean you should start writing with the introduction. Remember, the introduction is where the writer tells the reader what is going to be told to them. How do you know what you are going to tell them if you haven't written what the introduction references yet?

First, write the literature review. The literature review is the theory upon which your research population and data collection are built. Explain the theories used and how they interconnect if there is more than one theory. A dissertation literature review will be exhaustively extensive.

The literature review must be extensive because this is where a graduate student proves to the dissertation committee that the student understands the theory. They don't know that you know and understand the literature until they read the literature review. Yes, they know the literature, but you have to prove you know the literature, too. It will be heartbreaking when the literature review is chopped up to put in the first paper published from your dissertation, but such is the life of a graduate student and an upcoming academic.

Writing a literature review and methodology section. I'd stalled on my dissertation book project. When I realized writing about the literature review was the problem stopping me from writing the chapter on literature reviews, I had to laugh. I hated to write literature reviews and evidently, the distaste had transferred to writing about writing literature reviews. If you are in the same frame of mind, the literature review may also stall or be stalling your project.

After being in graduate school for three years or more and reading reams of other individuals' research, you know more than you think you do. What theories resonated with you? What type of research called to your personality? What questions need to be answered? Pull together, either physically or electronically, the titles of academic books and research papers that answer the above questions. How do they align themselves with the other theories in this pile? How do those titles align themselves with the research you want to do? Organize them in a pleasing way and make an argument.

Now write a paragraph or two explaining the reasons for this organization of the previous research and proposed method. Observe things missing in this previous research and explain how your project will illuminate what is missing. Now you have the beginning of a lit review.

Get outside help if needed. I wish I had had outside help with writing a literature review. Hire a coach, recruit a friend or a group of friends for support in pulling your literature review together. Writing a dissertation proposal or dissertation is often a lonely endeavor—call in support.

Write a rationale. The rationale should be obvious once you explain what is missing in past research around your topic. Show the research needs to be done because a phenomenon is unexplained and you are the perfect person to investigate it with a brilliant research design or a perfectly positioned occupation.

Generally, it isn't a bad idea to include why you are the best person to do this particular research. Maybe you have special access to a group of subjects that will help with the research. Perhaps you are a member of the study group. If these things are true, put them in the rationale. If your faculty advisor says to take this information out, then do so. Better to add things and then take them out, rather than leaving out something potentially useful.

For example, Mary Military's father was in the US Army. Her family moved from place to place around the world for most of her childhood. She understood the problems this caused her during that time. Changing schools and having to make new friends every two years was challenging. While the travel was amazingly enlightening, it was interpersonally difficult. For her dissertation, she wanted to use military families to examine how the constant moving shaped their family dynamics and communication. She still had connections to the military through her father, which gave her access to subjects to interview and fill out questionnaires. She used her experience and access as a reason for being the best person to do this research.

 **How can you leverage your experiences for being the best person to do your particular research?**

Know your methodology. Use the methodology that fits this research question. Don't be the person who knows only one way to do research. Remember the faculty member who gave the graduate students advice about favoring a methodology. It is like having a hammer making everything look like a nail. Sometimes you need a screwdriver and sometimes you need a saw. A hammer won't take a screw out, it will eventually break a piece of wood in half, and you'll have a holy mess.

Within reason, mold a research question towards a specific methodology, but be judicious when doing this. I doubt a faculty advisor will allow you to get too far into a proposal without vetting your research method. However, why look foolish when approaching your faculty advisor by not knowing everything about the chosen methodology?

Answer these questions about your methodology:

1. Why did you choose this method?

2. What kind of analysis do you plan to use on the data collected?

3. What are the shortcomings of this method and analysis?

4. How do you accommodate those shortcomings?

DEAR DISSERTATION WRITER

Pick the method best suited to this research. Understand it. Hopefully, you have used it in research papers in class and perhaps even in papers for conferences and maybe for publications. You will be discussing this methodology during both the proposal defense and the final dissertation defense.

Collect the data, do the analysis. Next, write about the collected data and tell about the analysis. Here are questions to get started (not an exhaustive list):

- Who were your subjects?
- How old were they?
- How did you contact them?
- Were they paid in cash or with Starbucks cards?
- If undergraduate students, did they get extra credit in a course for participation?
- Did you do interviews or questionnaires, or both?
- Did you use statistical analysis? If so, what kind?
- What do the results mean?

The data collection discussion may go in the methodology chapter. The analysis discussion will likely go in a separate chapter toward the end of the dissertation.

Now write the introduction. Only then go back and write the introduction because now you know what readers need to expect in future chapters. In other words, write in this order:

1. The literature review
2. Rationale
3. Methodology
4. Data collection
5. Analysis
6. Introduction

Remember the introduction you wrote for the proposal? Use this as a place to start, but now after writing the internal chapters, you know exactly what the reader needs to be told in the introduction.

Prepare a strong conclusion. Finally, write the conclusion, which is the *coup de gras* to the dissertation. In this section, bring home the best arguments for what these data mean. Also include a section explaining the limitations of this research, because no research is perfect.

For example, Mary Military did a qualitative study section of her dissertation explaining what being a military child looked like. Qualitative research is not generalizable, which is a limitation. The number of participants she used in her quantitative questionnaires, and therefore her analysis, wasn't as large as she would have liked. She had to explain how this low number occurred and mention this as a limitation. Further, she wrote about how much larger she would make her sample size in future research.

Mary Military wrote a section on future research following the limitations section, which she, or another researcher, could do in the future to compensate for the issues in gathering these data. She included new questions made clearer due to her analysis. New knowledge creates more questions. It is one of the things that makes science and research fun.

DEAR DISSERTATION WRITER

Dear Dissertation Writer,

I have described the structure of a social science dissertation or research paper. Remember the dissertation is a big research paper with an exhaustively extensive lit review. You can do this. First, breathe, and then type. Write a section at a time, revise it, and run it past your faculty advisor. Ready? Go!

Remember:

- ❏ Tell the reader what you want them to know three times.
- ❏ Don't write the intro first.
- ❏ Write the dissertation in this order:
  - ❏ Lit review
  - ❏ Rationale
  - ❏ Methodology
  - ❏ Data collection and analysis
  - ❏ Introduction
  - ❏ Conclusion

Section 3:
WHEN THE WRITING MUSE FLIPS YOU OFF

Chapter 10
SHHH... BUTT IN CHAIR TIME IS SACRED

> *I am always urging my students to honor their writing practice, to set up a schedule.*
>
> ~ Tayari Jones

I had a conversation with Steve Social-Star, a doctoral student client. He said, "I was looking at social media yesterday. It was a waste of time."

"Was this during your allotted dissertation writing time?"

"Yeah," he admitted.

"Yep, sounds like wasting valuable writing time. What do you want to do about it?"

"In the future, I'm going to look at social media only when I'm eating lunch."

"How can you be accountable for that pledge?" I asked.

"Well, I guess I could set a timer on my phone."

"Sounds like a plan," I said.

Social media isn't the problem. Timing is. Lunch is not writing time, so reading social media at lunch allows you to stay caught up on the activities of friends and family.

Put writing time on the calendar. My primary Get Your Dissertation Done strategy is what I call Sacred Dissertation Writing Time (SDWT), which is when *you* determine to write on the dissertation. One way to ensure writing gets done is to put writing times on a calendar, whether the times are for a half-hour or a four-hour block. By creating a schedule, you have told yourself and the universe about an intention to sit and write. Scheduling an intention makes it more likely you'll get butt in chair and fingers on keyboard. Planning to write during free time works about as well as saving the money left at the end of the month. There rarely is any left.

Decide how often and when to write. My second Get Your Dissertation Done strategy is for writers to interact with their dissertations at least five to six days during the week. There will be days when it's only thirty minutes and other days longer but plan to write most every day. Staying in touch with the dissertation keeps it fresh and prevents the time-wasting task of figuring out what you were trying to say the last time you visited the document.

I've talked to students who think if they do not have a full day to write, it isn't worthwhile. Wrong! Thirty minutes a day of writing, if it is uninterrupted, produces many words. Don't shy away from sequestering thirty minutes of writing if it is all you have available. Even thirty minutes will keep the flow of thoughts from getting stale.

Fifteen to thirty minutes is a minimum, but how about a maximum? Maybe you can sit in a chair for the whole day. I can't write that long and I don't recommend it. Neither would any physician or chiropractor. Ask them. After I've written for about two hours, I need to stop for a while and do something else. Get up and stretch every hour. Even my Fitbit reminds me I need to move during each waking hour.

Besides, toward the end of the dissertation writing, when you have an absolute deadline for turning in the final product, writing nonstop for an extended period of time may be required. Still, remember to stop at regular intervals and take a stretch break.

Cleaning house during writing time has gotten a bad rap in the procrastination literature. However, by cleaning the house during break time from writing, you can have a triple win. Writing gets done, your home is neater, AND your body gets a little workout, which gives your mind time to clear. Ain't nothin' wrong with that! Cleaning <u>instead</u> of writing though is not a good idea.

Other things to do to step away from the computer include a walk in the park, a shower, water the plants, prepare dinner, walk the dog, start a load of laundry, clear the sink of dirty dishes, or take a power nap (maximum thirty-minutes). After these kinds of breaks, you will be refreshed and feel much more like writing again.

Fay Focused-and-Quiet wrote her dissertation from 9:00 p.m. until 1:00 a.m. in the graduate student lounge after most students had gone home. It was quiet and she could use the university's computers furnished by the department. I was astounded because I could not write at that hour! My best four-hour writing stretch was from 8:00 a.m. until noon. The point is it worked for her. There's no right or wrong time. Figure out what works for you and use it. Authors who have written multiple books say a regular writing time is part of their routine. The important thing is to ensure writing gets <u>done</u>.

 **What will be your Sacred Dissertation Writing Time strategies?**

SHHH... BUTT IN CHAIR TIME IS SACRED

Protect this time. The time marked on your calendar must be considered *sacred*. Give up this time only if a loved one is in the hospital. When a friend calls and suggests coffee during SDWT, the correct answer is, "Sorry, I have something scheduled. How about another time?" Don't explain what is scheduled. Some friends will understand. Others will not and may try to undermine this dedication to writing. Don't give them the opportunity. "I have something scheduled" is a perfect answer to an invasion of Sacred Dissertation Writing Time.

 How can you protect this time? Who is most likely to invade it?

DEAR DISSERTATION WRITER

Invaders of Sacred Dissertation Writing Time. Other possible invaders of the SDWT are electronic. When you sit down to write, turn off the phone. If it has to be on, then at least silence it. Vow not to answer texts or return phone calls unless it fits into the above criterion to leave SDWT, i.e., a loved one in the hospital.

Turn off email. Quit the program. Those emails will not disappear because they've not been seen immediately. Turn off time-sucking social media sites and beloved apps, e.g., Facebook, Instagram, Twitter, YouTube, Tik-Tok, games, and podcasts (I'm sure there are others).

 **What time-sucking apps need to be turned off?**

SHHH... BUTT IN CHAIR TIME IS SACRED

Sacred Dissertation Writing Time is <u>writing time</u>. SDWT is not article reading time, not the time to find the pesky fact holding up an entire argument. During SDWT, if you vaguely remember an article that would fit this particular spot in the argument, mark the spot as a reminder to search later. Use **CHK** (stands for "check") for items you want to go back and update or confirm. Continue writing. Of course, you will need to read supporting information to complete the dissertation, but not during SDWT. Does it bear repeating? This is writing time only.

It is easy to get sidetracked by reading articles or researching for supporting facts. Before you know it, the writing time has disappeared. The urge to read or research is the CYH trying to distract you from writing. Don't give in to it.

Another way to enforce writing time is to set an alarm. The alarm on my phone goes off every day at 11:00 a.m. to remind myself to stop whatever I am doing and write a poem. It works for me, and hopefully, it will work for you. When taking a break, decide how long it will be and set a timer, especially when taking a power nap. It is easy to oversleep, set an alarm to wake up.

Consider this: I want to get something done the next day, such as writing. However, often intentions go by the wayside unless a plan is made. I find if I set a plan in my mind as I go to bed to write at 4:00 in the afternoon, it is easier to write because I have set the intention. Keep a notepad by your bed and note a plan to write the next day. Make a corresponding calendar entry and alarm. This sets you up for success and success is what we're after.

If something tangible works better for you, make a goals chart. On each day of writing, give yourself a checkmark, a gold star, or a sticker. Yeah, I know it sounds like kindergarten, but honestly, they give stars and stickers to kids because a little reward gives you a burst of dopamine. Looking at the chart with writing accomplishments on it will do the same. Earn end-of-day or end-of-week rewards when writing goals are achieved. Lastly, enlist a fellow graduate student to be an accountability partner. Share planned writing times and send text messages or email messages to each other. It is incredible how much will be accomplished if you tell someone.

 **Who could be your accountability partner?**

Managing others' expectations of your availability. Prepare the people who usually contact you by explaining the new time management process. Setting expectations goes a long way to not hurt someone's feelings when an email or text is not immediately answered.

If you are teaching, tell students there are times when you are unavailable to answer their incredibly important question, which is likely addressed in the syllabus. (Well, maybe don't use those terms.) Tell them, "I won't be available to answer emails (or texts, or however they contact you) until after 10:00 most mornings." Remind them you are also a student with an extensive writing project to complete. They like this kind of sharing and will appreciate you thought of them.

Tell friends and spouses, those who wish the best for you, what the specific offline times will be. Especially if they can't go ten minutes without sending a cute text or kitten memes. Promise to reply as soon as you return to the real world. They love you and setting expectations will help them understand why you don't LOL immediately to their every reaching out.

 **Who in your world needs expectations managed?**

Build in a day of rest. On the flip side, take at least one day a week off from writing. Play. Don't feel guilty about it. Brains need a break. However, have a way to record notes just in case inspiration hits during this day off.

Brains are funny things. While not consciously thinking about a dissertation issue while playing, your brain is working on it below conscious thought. Playtime is often when a brilliant idea pops into your head and solves all the dilemmas (well, maybe not all, but perhaps some). Write the genius idea down with some context.

I know you'll think your genius idea is the most memorable of thoughts because it truly is brilliant, but do not take a chance on memory. Write it down on a napkin or record it on your phone. Don't let it end up in the lost heap of other amazing thoughts not written down.

 **What day would you take off?**

SHHH... BUTT IN CHAIR TIME IS SACRED

These writing strategies will be helpful if you choose the life of a researcher. A researcher must be a writer because research not recorded and published is not shared. While I was in graduate school, I had a faculty member tell me her academic job became easier the day she realized she was a writer.

Remember Fay Focused-and-Quiet and what I thought were odd times to be writing? She finished her dissertation, defended it, and was offered a tenure-track position. I don't know if she still writes from 9:00 p.m. to 1:00 a.m., but it worked for her.

Dear Dissertation Writer,

Find a time that works for you, keep it sacred, and write on.

Remember:

- ❏ Put Sacred Dissertation Writing Time on a calendar.
- ❏ Beware of invaders! Protect Sacred Dissertation Writing Time.
- ❏ Don't research during writing times.
- ❏ Manage others' expectations during your writing times.
- ❏ Take a day off from writing. Not a week's vacation. Got it?

Chapter 11
YOU HAVE TO WRITE TO WRITE

I write to discover.

~ **Joe Henry, poet, and songwriter, January 2020 podcast,** *On Being*

The easiest thing to do on the earth is not write.

~ **William Goldman**

At the end of a coaching session with Amy Get-It-Right, I asked her about her plans for the next week. She said, "I've blocked out an hour on Monday, Wednesday, and Friday from 1:00 to 2:00 for writing and Tuesday, Thursday and Saturday from 10:00 to 11:00. I'm going to take Sunday off."

"Sounds like a plan," I said. The next week she came into my office and said, "I don't know what happened, but I didn't write all week. I couldn't make myself sit down and write."

What happened to her? She had her Sacred Dissertation Writing Times set up, but we had not talked about how to get herself to write during this time. Instead, she told me she thought about writing; she planned what she would write; and she researched what she needed to write. Sitting down to write? That was the real challenge.

 **What are your strategies?**

Write your thoughts. One of my favorite books about writing is *Bird by Bird* by Anne Lamott. Her advice is to sit down and write whatever comes into your head. She calls this her "shitty first draft." Her fear is she will leave her shitty first draft and die before revising it. She fears that others will read the unedited writing and say, "She wasn't a very good writer after all." Funny what the Committee in Your Head says about your writing process.

Writing your thoughts down as they come helps illuminate what you know and put them in order. Mental jumbled thoughts make organization or logic difficult to find. Once you write down those thoughts, you can determine whether or not they are logical. If they are not logical, writing them down exposes holes in the logic and perhaps provides a vision of how to fix the holes.

Write words in a row. Every book on writing I have read encourages writers (and you are a writer, you know) to put words on a page. Authors call the practice of putting the editor in the closet many different things. While Anne Lamott calls it her "shitty first draft," Clive Matson writes about letting the crazy child out. Betty Sue Flowers calls it the wild man. Notice none of these teachers of creativity name it something sane or calm. Writing what is in your imagination can be daunting. Whatever you call your creativity, let it out and write.

Sitting and writing can be scary. Tell the Committee in Your Head (CYH), "We are putting thoughts on a page, not writing." This first writing doesn't need to be clear or linear. Ways to put these first thoughts down include:

✓ Bullet points
✓ An outline
✓ A mind map
✓ Sticky notes

YOU HAVE TO WRITE TO WRITE

Perhaps promising you have to write for only fifteen minutes helps the CYH let you sit down to write. Pound keys or hold a pen or pencil over paper, but put words in a row...and – Voilà—writing!

Amy Get-It-Right reported to me she had sat down at her appointed writing time and then got up when her time was up with nothing on the page. I suggested she try these steps:

1. Start typing. She wailed, "But what do I write?"
2. I suggested she start where she left off the last time she wrote. If nothing comes to mind, start with, "I don't know what to type here. I'm frustrated with not being able to come up with a coherent sentence. If I were going to write anything, it would be about..."
3. See how this process works for you.

Write, don't research. Once you start writing, do not stop to go find a source. Put a note in this shitty, wild man, crazy child first draft what needs to be referenced, what brilliant person said this particular thing that is important to the argument. Research later. Remember to use **CHK** (stands for "check") where the reference needs to go and keep writing. Neither perfection nor completion is the aim right now. Don't get distracted by details. Let it be okay at this moment you can't recall the author's name or the article and move forward. This notation works well because a search will turn up very little else.

 **What do you need to do to write without revising?**

Write what you know. The first time you write about something, write what is already in your brain. Do not try to include academic-ese that doesn't come naturally. I've talked to students who get stressed about sounding smart and can't get out of their heads to deliver words to the page. If this happens, remember you will go back and make it sound "smarter" through revision. Right now, write what you know. Write it as if you are writing it to a program cohort member.

When I was first writing the last chapter of my dissertation, I was tired of writing. The only way I could get words on a page was to title my headings with annoyed-sounding titles. I wrote, "So if anyone cared about my research, what would I tell them about it?", which was the review. Another was titled, "What would I tell people is wrong with this research?" Also known as the limitations section. Of course, those section headings didn't stay with those titles, but they helped me to know what I was writing about and they made me smile. I wrote something. The same exercise might help you. Try using silly titles before your last chapter, you rebel, you.

Stop writing. Yes, you read correctly, stop before exhaustion sets in. I recommend stopping after about two to three hours of writing. If you stop when you hate writing, why would you want to come back to it? Upon coming to a frustrating place, write about the problem and stop. Come back to it more refreshed.

Ursula Uncertain came to my office one morning and said, "I stayed up way too late writing on my dissertation."

"Did you like any of the writing?" I asked.

"No, I looked at it this morning and most of what I wrote after I got tired, I won't be able to use."

"Huh, lesson learned?"

"Yeah, I'm going to quit after two or three hours. If I write when I'm tired, it ends up being garbage."

"I'm glad you figured it out."

YOU HAVE TO WRITE TO WRITE

 **When have you written too long? How did you feel? Where in your body did you feel it?**

Write, don't revise. When you sit down to write and have nothing to say, do not, I repeat, DO NOT, default to revising previous writings at this point. Instead, ask what needs to be written. What comes next?

Here is a list of the problems created when you revise too soon:
- Revising things that might change or get deleted later
- Perfecting a paragraph, you later no longer need
- Over-revising and losing a better draft
- Losing perspective on what's good
- Losing valuable writing time
- Suffering discouragement

Amy Get-It-Right was very proud of a paragraph in her literature review. She brought it into my office to read to me. It was indeed a lovely paragraph, clear and concise. She told me she'd written and rewritten it until it was perfect. The only problem was she came to see me weeks later and was despondent. She had to cut her perfect paragraph because her research had taken a different turn and the literature was no longer relevant to her writing. Major bummer!

Revise only after a large logical section is written. Stephen King, in his book *On Writing*, writes that his routine is to write the entire book before revising it. Then, he lets it sit in a drawer for six weeks. When he rereads it, he views the writing with fresh eyes and has a stronger ability to pay attention to what works and what doesn't, such as which storylines are complete or which need deletion or embellishment.

You may not want to do this with your dissertation. Faculty advisors want to see progress on each chapter. However, the general practice -- not reading your writing until you've completed a large section or chapter -- works well. What needs to be revised is not often clear until a section or an argument is finished.

What is the Committee in Your Head telling you about writing without revising until you have a large enough section to revise?

Leave notes. This strategy may appear to be counter-intuitive, but stop when writing is going well. The question then arises: How do I know what to write the next day? Leave "breadcrumb" notes before closing the document for the day. Type questions you want to answer or a statement to address in the next pages.

Curt Competent was writing his literature review. He had made a list of the articles he wanted to explain before he started writing. As he addressed each one, he checked them off the list. When he had described them all, he left himself a note to tell his future reader how his research questions would influence the theories he'd discussed. By leaving himself notes, he had a place to start when he returned to the document. This kept him from going back over what he had already written, which often leads to revising.

 **What kinds of notes could you leave yourself at the end of a writing session?**

What do you want your experience to be? When Fay Focused-and-Quiet started writing her dissertation, she talked about writing and her plans for writing, such as putting it on her calendar. The next two or three times we met, she had reasons why she hadn't written—work, illness, car repairs. She knew what she wanted to write, and was able to articulate it to me, but she didn't do it. She was very frustrated. I questioned her about her thoughts when it came time for her to write, and she realized she was listening to the CYH. It stopped her from writing. At her next coaching session, she told me what changes she had made:

- She looked up daily affirmations and posted the ones she liked on her mirror, sink, and refrigerator door.
- She set daily timers on her electronic devices to nudge her to her computer.
- Once seated in front of her computer, she set a 30-minute timer. When it went off, she asked herself whether she felt like writing longer? If not, she stopped.
- She wrote herself notes before she left the computer about what to write next.
- She had fun creating and highlighting goofy subheads for sections in her first draft.
- She rewarded herself for a daily "to-do" well done with a cappuccino.
- She took a walk in the fresh air, which was a great way to stretch a stiff, hunched-over-a-computer body.

During a coaching session, Amy Get-It-Right told me she was amazed at how good a specific chapter turned out. She wrote it over several days and set it aside. Upon rereading the completed chapter, she decided it was not precisely what she wanted to say. She then rewrote it several times and was happier with her revision. Note the steps she took:

- She completed the first draft of her chapter (or section).
- She put the chapter (or section) aside for several days.
- She reread what she had written.

- She decided if the content focused, supported, and delivered what she wanted to say.
- She revised problem sections (or paragraphs) to complete a final draft.

I told her she got there because she completed her first draft; then, kept writing until her work matured into what it needed to become. Revise, until it expresses precisely what you want it to say. Thinking about it won't get it done. Writing will.

Remember writing is putting words in a row (a sensible row). It is not revising or researching. Remember no one will see this draft. Let it be as shitty or wild or crazy as anything ever written. It will be cleaned up later to be a nice shiny academic chapter. Later.

Help is out there. The wonderful addition to our lives, the Internet (oh yeah, some of you have had it your entire lives) offers innumerable resources to those looking for writing tips. There are organizations (Writers' Digest, Writers' League of Texas, Book Baby), blogs, editor and agent websites, and university and nonprofit websites with writing tips (OWL, the Purdue Online Writing Lab). Sites that answer writing questions are numerous (Grammarly). Edge towards sites with large followings, because people vote with their presence on websites that have value. You can trust you will get good advice from popular sites. But don't let this be a suck on your writing time. It is much more fun to research writing than to do it, isn't it?

Dear Dissertation Writer,

Write now! Tap, tap, tap. Click those keys for the win. Yay!

Remember:

❏ Write out thoughts for them to become clear.

❏ Writing is putting words in a logical order.

❏ Write without revising.

- ❏ Revise only after a large, logical section is completed.
- ❏ Write without researching (insert **CHK** to locate resources later)
- ❏ Stop writing while it's going well, before exhaustion sets in.
- ❏ Leave notes for what to write in your next writing session.

Chapter 12
OH, YEAH? PROVE IT

Why do I have to write a dissertation?

~ Ursula Uncertain

She came into my office and asked the above question. Those of us who have written one, are in the middle of one, or are staring into the dissertation writing future, ask this reasonable question. Or maybe this was not a question for you. All you knew was it was the last hoop to getting a doctoral degree. This chapter is to answer the "why" question.

 **Why did you want to go to graduate school?**

What courses did you take? In my doctoral program, I took forty-five hours of coursework post-master's degree. At three hours per course and nine hours per semester, I took fifteen courses. Within those fifteen courses, I chose to take (with the approval of my faculty advisor) courses such as *Theories of Interpersonal Communication, Ethnography of Speaking, Social Psychology and Family, Qualitative Research Methods*, and *Quantitative Research Methods*.

Your academic requirements may be similar to mine or vastly different. Students in my department interested in quantitative research took at least nine hours of statistics coursework. My assumption is your courses were theory and methods courses relevant to your area of study and particular research interests to teach you how to do research.

Why does coursework matter? You most likely learned what a theory is and the different theories relevant to a field of study. Learning how theory is developed and expanded, and how experts use those theories is critical to becoming a scholar. Perhaps some of those theories have since been disproven but were theories accepted by experts previously. Coursework introduced different research methods and there were various methods you liked. By reading and studying journal articles, instructors and professors taught how experts in your specific area present research papers in journals. Hopefully, those who taught you expected actual research from their students. The culmination of everything your professors taught you is demonstrated by the research and writing in your dissertation.

How did you feel about learning how to do research?

OH, YEAH? PROVE IT

The real reason to write a dissertation. Why graduate students write dissertations: to prove to the graduate student, a faculty advisor, an academic committee, and through them, the department, the university, and perhaps to the academic world, that the student knows how to do high quality, in-depth original research independently. The portions of this statement worth parsing out are:

1. Prove to these various entities
2. Understanding how to do high quality, in-depth, original research
3. Complete research independently

Graduate students write dissertations *to prove to various entities* they know how to research independently. The thought of proving something to these people may be paralyzing. The CYH reminds you of doubts and fears about worthiness and ability. Original research requires becoming vulnerable to people who are experts in their fields.

Most of the people on a dissertation committee will have written dissertations of their own, have tenure track professions at research universities, and have published countless articles in peer-reviewed journals. When thinking of the expertise in this group, the CYH will say, "Who are you to think you could join their ranks?" or "Quit now before they discover you're a fraud."

Do not listen to the CYH! It is a liar. It aims to keep you safe, but in the end, it will only make you small. Think big. The department and your faculty advisor believe you can do this or they would not have taken you on as a student. Believe them. Remind the CYH you are an adult now. Here are some possible steps:

- Write down the most negative fear. Safely burn or shred it.
- Record this pep talk and play it back to yourself: *You can handle pressure and even possible rejection because you are doing high-quality, in-depth, original work. And I am proud of you!*
- Repeat the above affirmation out loud in front of a mirror every morning.

After I'd finished my degree, a graduate student at a conference asked who had been on my committee. After hearing the names, she said, "Wow, those are some pretty impressive names." Yes, they were.

Suddenly the knowledge struck me with a kind of backward anxiety. Maybe I should have been more impressed at the time by the people on my committee. Luckily, I had not thought of it before my defense. They were simply the people with whom I had taken coursework and had supported me throughout my graduate student days.

Proving you can do *high-quality, in-depth original research* is another reason graduate students are required to write dissertations. By writing one, you prove you are qualified to claim to be a researcher.

I hear the CYH saying, "Yeah, but this is much bigger." Yes, it is bigger AND you can do it. Remind the CYH of this:

- I wrote research papers in my classes.
- I presented my papers at conferences (if you have not, maybe you should try).
- I came to graduate school to learn how to do research.
- I know how to do research.

Don't chicken out now. Don't let the CYH get you down!

How do you feel about writing a dissertation?

OH, YEAH? PROVE IT

Further, remember your dissertation is not the culmination of an academic career. This research and writing are only the beginning. Try not to put pressure on yourself to write a groundbreaking, world-exploding, theory-bending piece of research. Of course, everyone wants to advance theory—that is what makes it original—but no one expects a graduate student to put the academic world on its ear. Now making a big splash would be fun; do it if the research takes you there, but it is not the purpose of the dissertation. Originate an idea about a topic you like, that can be justified, needs to be explored, is manageable, advances theory, and is doable in a reasonable amount of time.

It will be in-depth because graduate students must convince these entities they know the following things:

- A particular subject in depth
- What theories apply to this subject
- How those theories intersect and contradict
- Where this research fits in the panoply of theories
- How to explain a particular method(s) in the same depth
- Why this method is the best methodology for this piece of research
- What other methods could have been used, but were not chosen and why.

Explain the above and then a dissertation committee knows you learned and understood the information they taught you because you showed your knowledge of theories and methodology in painful depth in your dissertation. Likely you'll never need to write this in-depth again because readers of journal articles and academic books know the background. It will cause great pain when you start cutting down your dissertation to publish it and have to take out the things you explained with incredible clarity because the journal or book readers know them, too.

Don't let the term "high-quality research" get you down, either. A faculty advisor will hold you to the standard to fit your department. Do NOT compare any early writing to another's finished dissertation. Even Curt Competent fell for this one. He came to my office and said:

"I'm depressed. I read Emily Amazing's completed dissertation in the library. I doubt mine will ever read like hers."

"Curt," I said. "How many times do you think she revised her dissertation before it landed on the library shelf? I promise Emily Amazing rewrote it countless times after her faculty advisor gave her feedback. Of course, your writing, in the beginning, isn't going to sound perfect. For all we know, she may have hired an editor, too."

Any early writing is not going to be as smooth or knowledgeable as a finished piece. Remember small steps, and early writing will end up as good as the finished dissertation in the library. One more revision and it will be there. (Well, maybe several revisions, but you know what I mean.) Trust your faculty advisor with ensuring it is good enough.

The purpose of a dissertation is to prove to these entitles a graduate student can do in-depth, high-quality research independently. You will do the following.

- ✓ Create a question you want to research.
- ✓ Research to write the literature review.
- ✓ Choose what methodology will best answer your question.
- ✓ Collect the data, analyze it, and interpret what it means.

However, remember you are not totally on your own. Graduate schools give students the support of faculty advisors and academic committee members to shepherd them through this process. They want graduate students to swim, not drown. They will be there if you feel you're sinking. Do your part of the work and allow them to help when you feel underwater.

In summary, the reason graduate students write a dissertation is to show various academic people in an institution that they have taught the student well enough to do research independently in the manner expected by graduate faculty. Once you have proven you can do research on your own, you will be a proud alumnus of your institution and in a long line of academics who have gone through this trial by fire, emerging in the end, perhaps somewhat battered, but triumphant.

 **How do you feel about the reasons stated here for writing a dissertation?**

Dear Dissertation Writer,

The goal of becoming a researcher and possibly an academic is the reason you went to graduate school. Remind yourself of those reasons when the CYH starts giving you grief wondering what the heck you are doing!

Remember:

- ❏ Graduate students write a dissertation to prove to themselves, their advisors, their departments, and to the academic world that the student has learned how to do high-quality, in-depth, original research mostly independently.

Section 4:
SHOWTIME

Chapter 13
THE ANXIETY IS ALMOST OVER

Five faculty members deciding your fate. What could go wrong?

~ Unknown graduate student

Any committee that is the slightest use is composed of people who are too busy to want to sit on it for a second longer than they have to.

~ Katharine Whitehorn

Mary Military rushed into my office. "My advisor approved my dissertation draft and said I could set up a final defense meeting!"

"Congratulations!" I said. "I'm excited for you."

"Now what?" she asked.

I told her it was time to prep for that dissertation defense. She had gathered and analyzed data, written up her results, and done the heavy lifting. She and her faculty advisor had traded the final dissertation several (yeah, probably more) times and worked out any remaining problems the two of them had found. Now the big day had arrived. It was time to meet with her committee and officially defend her finished dissertation. The following are suggestions to smooth the path to an exciting day.

Double-check that your paperwork is in order. Setting a date and getting paperwork (or online documentation) in order is essential. Amy Get-it-Right followed the bureaucratic steps for setting up her dissertation defense, which were:

- ✓ Read the graduate school website information about defenses
- ✓ Downloaded the correct forms
- ✓ Got the necessary signatures or online approvals
- ✓ Turned in the forms within the time frame required by the graduate school

These days much of this is probably handled online and isn't particularly difficult. Nevertheless, know your graduate school's requirements for a student planning a dissertation defense. Look it up. Do it correctly. When it came time for Amy's dissertation defense, her faculty advisor had the paperwork she needed from the graduate school when the committee met.

Steve Social-Star set the date with his committee. On the day of the meeting, Steve's faculty advisor did not have the necessary paperwork for the committee to sign if, and when, the committee approved his dissertation, which was becoming a bigger "if" by the minute. His faculty advisor realized the error on the day of the defense and contacted me, the departmental graduate coordinator.

"He has no graduate school defense paperwork. What do I do now? His committee meets in an hour," he said.

Luckily for Steve, it was summer and a slow time at the graduate school and my office. I walked across campus to the Graduate School. "He what? And you're here saving his butt at the eleventh hour?" was the silent response burning through the scolding eyes of the grad school employees.

Believe me, my blood pressure and I blamed the glaring error on the student. We discussed how amazed we were that students don't research to determine what bureaucratic things they need to do to defend the most important document of their graduate careers.

I got the paperwork done. Had the defense been scheduled for another time of the year, Steve's advisor might have had to cancel the meeting. Then Steve would have had to get the graduate school's paperwork requirements met. Only after doing the paperwork correctly could he schedule another meeting. Imagine how unhappy his committee members would have been to have to return weeks later to discuss his dissertation. Don't start a dissertation defense with an angry, disappointed committee.

I walked the paperwork back to the building where Steve and his committee were meeting. It turned out okay, but Steve put himself, and a handful of staffers, including me, under unnecessary pressure. His faculty advisor and I could have instead spent our time and effort emotionally supporting him.

"Steve, what were you thinking?" I asked.

"No one told me how to set up a meeting and I didn't think to ask," he said. "I heard you set up a meeting and then you meet."

Learn from Steve's mistake, and check to find out if there are express requirements for setting up a dissertation defense.

What are the requirements of your graduate school for setting up a dissertation defense meeting?

Reread your dissertation. A few days or, at a minimum, the day before the defense, reread your dissertation. I know you are probably sick to death of it by this time, but read it one more time. Try to read it as if it were fresh. What are the questions one might ask about a document of this kind? Try to prepare answers to those questions. Departments have different formats for dissertation defenses; some require a presentation of the research, which provides a useful review of the material beforehand.

Many students have been lucky enough to have job interviews during which they presented their dissertation research, and thereby gained a good idea of the questions listeners ask about their material. If you've not had interviews, do a presentation before peers and find out what questions they have about this research.

What questions might faculty members ask? Consider committee members' research interests along with any research quirks they have. If you are not familiar with a member, use your research skills and ask your network about odd characteristics. Think of what this project might spark in their minds. Be prepared for these possibilities.

What questions might come up from your committee?

Ask your faculty advisor if she has thoughts on questions she expects from the committee. I failed to ask my advisor. After my stressful defense was over and we talked about the first problematic question I'd received, she commented, "I thought that might come up." I had not asked her what she thought might come up, and she had not thought to prepare me for the possibility. Learn from my mistake. Ask your faculty advisor what questions the committee members might ask.

 **What has your advisor suggested are questions to expect at the defense?**

What time should the defense be? The time of day could be significant. If at all possible, schedule it for early in the morning or late in the afternoon. Early mornings are good because most people are at their sharpest. Late afternoon is good because everyone will have had a full day and will probably want to get the meeting done and go home.

However, given this advice, consider your circadian rhythms. The problem with late afternoon meetings is, of course, you're faced with an empty day with time to think of all that might go wrong. Try not to freak out before the meeting. If your brain does not work after lunch, try to have a morning meeting. If you are not a morning person, try to avoid scheduling a meeting then.

 **What time of day might be best for you to schedule a dissertation defense?**

Make a plan for the day. When I was the graduate coordinator, I'd try to visit with the students waiting for their meetings to begin. I hoped to distract them from their pre-defense jitters. If the meeting is in the afternoon, make a plan for the morning. Meet friends for breakfast or lunch or have something planned to fill the time. Studies have shown, when a person's blood is full of cortisol and adrenaline from stress, critical thinking is fuzzy. Work out in the morning, if possible, to burn off those stress hormones and clear up the brain. Come up with a plan. Don't let the day evolve by itself or you may arrive as a ball of anxiety at the defense.

Don't forget to sleep. Get as good a night's sleep as possible. Yes, it is a big day and for that reason, you want to be as sharp as you can be. If sleep is a problem, research sleep hygiene to find hints for making sleeping easier.

Prepare for a post-defense letdown. When the meeting is over, regardless of the outcome, don't be surprised at how you feel. After my defense, I wanted to be excited and pleased I had passed but instead felt bludgeoned and stomped on. My best friend drove in from Dallas to have lunch with me. Thank goodness for her. She was a soul saver.

While I was working as the graduate coordinator, a graduate student came to my office after her defense. I closed the door and she cried nonstop for thirty minutes. Yes, she had passed and this was her way of releasing the stress emotions. I was happy to provide a safe place for her to do it. Having a plan for the post-defense time is important.

THE ANXIETY IS ALMOST OVER

 **What is your post-defense plan?**

Dear Dissertation Writer,

Time for the defense! You have prepared, you have rested, you have worked out, and you are ready! Take a deep breath and go impress the hell out of those faculty committee members (yeah, the committee in your head, too)!

Remember:

- ❑ Check with the department and graduate school about rules for setting up a defense meeting.
- ❑ Review the dissertation and ask your advisor for potential questions the committee might ask.
- ❑ Have a plan for dissertation defense day (before and after the defense).
- ❑ Practice health. Sleep, exercise, and eat something before the meeting.

Chapter 14
MY TALE OF TWO COMMITTEES

At my dissertation defense, I knew I'd be dealing with the faculty committee who would tell me whether my years of work for a doctoral degree had been in vain or not. What I had not expected was dealing with the second committee, the one in my head.

I started graduate school in Communication Studies at age forty as an answer to a mid-life crisis. Seven years later, I faced the final challenge of my graduate program, the dreaded doctoral dissertation defense. Sitting before a committee of five august professors to defend my research was the culmination of the doctoral journey. Generally, I don't think well under pressure and this was going to be the most pressure-filled day of my life. The Committee in Your (My) Head (CYH) was engaged in a rousing conversation of recriminations and fears.

The meeting was set for Friday, August 28, 1998, at 10:00 a.m. in the Dean's Conference Room. Usually, these meetings were held in the conference room within the departmental office. However, due to scheduling issues (yay), I had to reserve the Dean's Conference Room with big rolling chairs around a large glass-topped table and portraits of dour former deans on the walls.

I arrived early. The graduate student convention was to bring snacks and drinks for the committee. You want these people to be happy with you when they sit down to talk about this project. Nothing says "be happy" like snacks. I brought bagels, muffins, chocolate kisses, water, and Einstein Brothers' coffee. I set the table with the food nicely displayed on a platter with plates and napkins handy.

I brought a paper copy of my dissertation, with notes in the margins I had made the night before. I'd given the faculty committee their hard copies two weeks prior as per Graduate School regulation. They had likely read it the night before too.

My advisor, Dr. Qualitative Research, arrived first. What a relief to see her friendly face. I was getting tense and sweaty from the CYH reminding me of the dire things to come. The rest of the academic committee

MY TALE OF TWO COMMITTEES

filed into the room. First, gruff Dr. Nonverbal Communication arrived. Throughout my graduate student years, the other professors had told the graduate students to call them by their first names, but not him. He dressed in his usual button-down shirt with gray jeans and running shoes. The CYH turned up the stress level upon his arrival.

Dr. Conversation Analysis followed him, dressed in a warm-up suit. Sad to say, he was battling colon cancer at the time of my defense and died in December of the same year. Seeing him looking gaunt and frail caused me to appreciate his attendance at my meeting.

Dr. Emotion-in-Communication, the other female committee member, arrived in her trim black skirt and dark lilac matching sweater set. Her kind and supportive nature caused the CYH to relax a little with her arrival.

Last, Dr. Anthropologist came in. I'd taken several classes with him and enjoyed them. He was one of the foremost experts in his field, the Ethnography of Speaking. "What were you thinking inviting someone of his caliber to be on your dissertation committee?" the CYH shrieked.

Most of the committee members were in their fifties. At least I assumed they were older than me except for young Dr. Emotion-in-Communication.

DEAR DISSERTATION WRITER

The committee settled in the big comfy chairs and sent me out of the room. Doing this was routine in dissertation defenses in my department. In the student's absence, the committee members discuss the work at hand. They decide whether or not the research is acceptable and who is going to ask what questions. If I had been in the conference room in the departmental office, I would have had friendly staff members around to encourage and remind me to breathe. Instead, I stood in an empty corridor with the CYH telling me the people inside the room hated my dissertation and I was going to fail.

Finally, Dr. Qualitative Analysis, my advisor, called me back into the room. I sat at the head of the long table and readied myself for the first question. Dr. Anthropologist asked, "What makes you think this is an Ethnography of Speaking?" Uhhh… I froze. I didn't think it was. I had tried to mold it into an Ethnography of Speaking because, at the proposal meeting, my faculty committee thought it was the best way for me to go. Of course, Dr. Anthropologist had not been at the meeting. I fumbled the answer and the CYH started yammering at me. The first question and I had screwed it up!

Each of the faculty members in turn asked their list of questions about my research. I don't recall other questions. I do remember Dr. Nonverbal Communication asked hard questions I wasn't sure I answered well. After the meeting was over, I thought of an answer to one of his questions. It was a good answer, too, but too late. I felt like Dr. Conversation Analysis was mean, which was likely his illness speaking. Dr. Emotion-in-Communication was nice, thank goodness. My advisor did her best to give me leading suggestions. In the midst of one of my long silences, she said to me, "Don't you remember we discussed that?" Oh, yeah, I remembered and answered the question. After an hour of grilling, they thanked me and told me to wait outside again.

I went into the empty hallway and sat hunched on the top step of a decorative stairway. With my elbows on my knees and my face in my hands, the CYH began to berate me.

"I don't think you gave one smart answer to any question!" "You sounded like an idiot in there!" "I can't believe how badly that went!"

I began to cry. At first, it was a sniffle or two and then tears started running down my face. I tried hard not to sob out loud. The CYH convinced me I had done the worst dissertation defense in the history of defenses. The years of my hard work had been for nothing.

Finally, the conference door opened. My advisor stepped out and said, "Congratulations, Dr. Corbin."

What?! Did I hear correctly? <u>Doctor</u> Corbin?! Well, that turned on the tears. I was sobbing as I walked into the conference room. I sat down in a chair and attempted to stop crying.

Soon the committee members were up and moving out of the room. By this time, I had stifled the tears and stood up. Dr. Nonverbal Communication and Dr. Conversation Analysis took turns hugging me as they left. Dr. Emotion-in-Communication said, "At least you didn't cry or throw up <u>during</u> the meeting."

"That happens?" I asked.

She nodded in the affirmative.

Oh, my. Hearing it made me feel better.

I stayed in the conference room with my advisor after they left. She had an itemized list of the things the committee wanted me to change in the dissertation. Thank goodness she'd kept track of what they wanted. She said they had signed the paperwork and were not interested in seeing the changes. Wow! She gave me the signature pages to be submitted to the Graduate School when I turned in the revised dissertation. Then she hugged me and was off. I could not believe it. The CYH had convinced me I'd failed. They were wrong.

I had prearranged an after-dissertation-defense lunch date with Anne, my graduate school friend. She drove more than three hours to be with me. Two months earlier, she had defended her dissertation with a few of the same faculty members and had a similar experience to mine. She understood what it was like to face the two committees (the faculty committee and the one in your head) and live to tell about it. We talked for over two hours about everything, sharing how horrible it had been for us, and how miraculous it was we'd passed. I appreciated she had felt as stupid and unable to answer questions during her defense as I had. She helped me put my heart and soul back together. It had been the worst and most memorable day of my life, which ended with the loving balm of friendship.

Chapter 15
YOU DESERVE TO CELEBRATE!

Graduation is an exciting time. It marks both an ending and a beginning; it's warm memories of the past and big dreams for the future.

~ Unknown

When Curt Competent finished his dissertation, he was tired of academia, which made the thought of going through the graduation ceremony exhausting. He said to me, "Why bother? It's a bunch of speeches and people dressed up in make-believe clothes. I'm tired of it."

Then there is the other group (including me) who want the hoopla.

Where's the hoopla? When I turned in the final copy of my dissertation (this was back in the day when students had to turn in a physical copy to the graduate school office), I went to the employee in charge of checking each student's formatting. She pulled out her ruler and checked the margins on several different pages. Honestly, she did! She checked: the title page making sure it read as it should; the correct signatures from my faculty committee; and, the page numbering. Finally, she said I had done everything I needed to do and congratulated me on completing the last hurdle to my graduate degree.

 **What are the rules at your Graduate School for turning in the dissertation?**

YOU DESERVE TO CELEBRATE!

While I appreciated her congratulations, I remember walking out of the building feeling like the moment was anticlimactic. After my hard work, I wanted confetti and balloons. I wanted cheering crowds and friendly pats on the back. I wanted some hoopla, damn it! I wasn't going to get it at the graduate office where they see one doctoral dissertation after another. For them, it was another day at the office.

Where to get your hoopla? At the graduation ceremony! It's where the hoopla starts. You wear doctoral regalia that have not changed since the medieval period. Academics wore the long heavy gowns to stay warm in drafty 13th-century stone buildings. They carried their lunches in the gown's long sleeves because they had no pockets. You think the academic system is feudal? It is! Universities formed in the Middle Ages haven't changed much in the current era. Think of graduation as academic dress-up.

What kind of regalia do you want to wear?
Is there something specific for your school?

I wrote this chapter before the Coronavirus pandemic and revised it during the shutdown. I witnessed disappointed graduates on television, including high school, undergraduate, and graduate students. Most schools attempted a ceremony through social media, such as Zoom graduations. The students still got to hear a commencement speech or two. At the University of Texas at Austin's graduation ceremony in 2020, the Graduate School allowed students to send pictures of themselves dressed in their regalia and send a recording of their names to help them be pronounced correctly. I'm sure the staff at the Graduate School was as disappointed as the students.

If it's a typical year, graduate students and faculty get dressed up. Family and friends attend. Graduate students file in and speeches are made. Hopefully, they will be uplifting and, maybe, even funny speeches. The Dean calls your name. Time to smile! As you walk across the stage, shake hands with the Dean and get a picture snapped by the professional photographer. Continue across the stage for congratulations from a departmental representative, maybe a handshake or a hug from your faculty advisor. Hear those friends and family in the audience whooping and hollering regardless of instructions to "please hold applause until all graduates have been named." Family and friends will take and share pictures of you dressed in regalia. This is the hoopla and it's worth attending the ceremonies because you deserve the hoopla. You worked long and hard on this graduate degree and a celebration is in order. Now that we have a vaccine, my hope is for a return to this kind of ceremony.

Have a party. Hopefully, you make plans for after the ceremony. I had a party at my house and invited my family and friends. I didn't want to deal with keeping food and drinks on the table so I had it catered. (I deemed it worth the splurge.) You may go to a restaurant and have a nice lunch or dinner. I had the party at my house because I wanted to wear my regalia during the party. My hope for you is a celebration most pleasing to you.

YOU DESERVE TO CELEBRATE!

 Remember to be polite and send out "Thank You" notes for any gifts received. Have you bought yours yet?

Harken back to the first chapter when I explained what the three letters in PhD could stand for? I want to add one more word.

The "D" in PhD stands for Done! Yes, you can do it. You proved it by doing the coursework and the comprehensive exams. You proved it by doing research papers. You will prove it by writing this dissertation. Imagine the final period on the last page. Imagine not having to write another tuition check. Imagine walking across the stage and shaking all those hands. Use these images to pull you to the writing and dissertation finish line.

 **What career do you wish to pursue? Are you going to teach in academia? You know you don't have to, but that's another book.**

Dear Dissertation Writer,

In Chapter 1 I said PhD stands for Persistence, humbling and hard, and Determination. Now the D stands for Done. I envision the future of a finished doctorate for you. Now, go do it!

Remember:

❏ Go to the graduation ceremony.

❏ Have a party.

❏ Celebrate this achievement.

❏ The "D" in PhD stands for "Done."

The End

ACKNOWLEDGMENTS

Anyone who has written something this long including a dissertation knows that you didn't write it alone. Sometimes it felt that way, but being social creatures as we are, we didn't do it alone. I want to thank the many people who supported me throughout this endeavor. These of course are not in any ranked order. That would be impossible. Also, I apologize if I've left anyone out. Forgive me.

I want to thank Carolyn Scarborough (carolynscarborough.com), creative coach extraordinaire without whom this would never have been finished. Her inviting me to her Beta creatives coaching group lit a fire under my butt to get this thing done. In December of 2019, she asked, "So Susan, how is that dissertation book going?" I had all but dropped it at that point. I'm so glad she got me back on track.

The members of the group (in alphabetical order because there is no ranking how wonderful they are) Julie Anderson, Jeanne Guy, Jan Myers, and Cynthia Treglia read countless versions of this book and made such incredible suggestions for changes. Beyond that, they listened to me complain about the problems I was having writing it. They nodded sagely and expected me to get back to it. Thanks so much, ladies.

Another writing group (I call it the Prose Critique Group) to which I belong also read various versions of the chapters. The membership has seen a rotation of members, so not all of these people are in the group now, but many of them read portions of the book over the years of my writing it. My fervent thanks go to Shelley Pernot, Gina Harlow, Teresa Bitner, Cassie Wedding, Carrye Franzell, Gerry Tucker, Cindy Marabito, Rachel Starnes, and Michelle Hefner.

Janine Dworin who designed the drawings in this book has to be mentioned. Currently, she is a master's student in vocal performance at the University of North Texas in Denton. Her mother, Diana Dworin goes to the same small faith community where I go. She posted some of her daughter's drawings on Facebook and I thought, "I'll bet she could draw some stick figures for me." She outdid all my expectations. The little stick figure on the back of the book dressed in doctoral robes and yelling

"Done" was all her conception. I suggested a figure throwing a tam in the air; she put the robes on it. I loved it at first sight.

The editors I paid to go through the work were invaluable. Karen Aeorin suggested the current title and that I flesh out the characters more. Now they seem like real people to me. Terri Schexnauder helped find the many typos and needed commas throughout the pages. My unpaid editor, grammar perfectionist, and long-time friend did the last proofread for me. Thank you, Cathy Williamson.

The critiques by Adria Battalia and Kerk Kee, former doctoral students from UT whom I coached were valuable to the work and to my desire to keep writing. Never underestimate how important it is to a writer to tell them that the work is valuable.

Have you checked out my coaching website? I have Karie Williams (KarieWilliams.com) to thank for how wonderful it looks and Riley Blanks (wokebeauty.com) for the amazing photography there.

I love the work of my book designer, Roberta Morris (leaveittoberta.com). Looks lovely, doesn't it?

Finally, I want to thank my family. My husband of many years, John Corbin sat through countless conversations of my wondering what the heck I thought I could say in a book such as this. As well as my finding one more thing to spend money on for a self-published book. Who knew? I do now. My grown children and their spouses, Mark and Valerie Corbin and Becky and Kevin Peek, have supported their mother thinking she is an author. They are rather used to me reinventing myself every twenty years or so.

To all the hard-working graduate students and faculty members through the years that have taught me what I wrote here, I also owe deep gratitude. The book wouldn't exist were it not for you.

Thank you, thank you, thank you. (Thanks, Anne Lamott)

August 2021

ABOUT THE AUTHOR

Susan D. Corbin graduated from the Communication Studies Department at the University of Texas with a master's and a doctorate. She is a life coach specializing in helping graduate students finish their graduate programs. She worked at the University of Texas in student support for fifteen years and is now retired. Currently, she has her own coaching practice and has written a book for students entitled *Dear Dissertation Writer: Stories, Strategies, and Self-Care Tips to Get Done*.

www.ingramcontent.com/pod-product-compliance
Lightning Source LLC
Chambersburg PA
CBHW072202100526
44589CB00015B/2333